S0-BCW-508

Hasena Thomas

Hasena Thomas

Hasena Thomas

Hasena Thomas

Hasena Thomas

Cameron
Daley

Cameron Daly

Turee Coburn

Becoming Like Him

God's Reflection

Produced under the auspices of the
Office of Education
North American Division of the
General Conference of Seventh-day Adventists

Pacific Press® Publishing Association
Nampa, Idaho

Copyright © 2007 by the Office of Education
North American Division of the
General Conference of Seventh-day Adventists
Silver Spring, MD 20904-6600

CONTENTS

■ Unit 1: Who Is God?

Lesson 1	An Ancient Book Written for You	6
Lesson 2	God's Word in Human Languages	14
Lesson 3	Always There Is God	24
Lesson 4	"If You Have Seen Me . . ."	30
Lesson 5	A Comforter Is Sent	36

■ Unit 2: Changing to Become Like God

Lesson 6	They Spoke for God	44
Lesson 7	Sin Is More Than Something I Do	52
Lesson 8	The Problem of Guilt	60
Lesson 9	A New Heart	68
Lesson 10	Faith: Taking God at His Word	74
Lesson 11	Keeping in Touch With God	80
Lesson 12	God Is on Our Side	88

■ Unit 3: Getting to Know God

Lesson 13	Two Men: Two Decisions	96
Lesson 14	The Gospel According to Mary	102
Lesson 15	The Power of Love	110
Lesson 16	"Stay With Us"	116

■ Unit 4: Choosing God

Lesson 17	The Gospel According to You	126
Lesson 18	What Makes You "You"?	134
Lesson 19	The Healthy Christian	140
Lesson 20	You Are Special to Him	146

■ Unit 5: Understanding God

Lesson 21   Tell It to the World   156

Lesson 22   Seventh-day Adventists Believe   164

Lesson 23   A Time to Rejoice   174

Lesson 24   A New Life in Christ   182

Lesson 25   In Remembrance of Me   188

Lesson 26   When Death Comes to the Christian   194

Lesson 27   Windows of Heaven   200

■ Unit 6: Sharing God

Lesson 28   What Is a Family?   210

Lesson 29   What Is a Friend?   218

Lesson 30   What Is a Church?   226

Lesson 31   Your House Is the World   232

■ Unit 7: Becoming Like Him

Lesson 32   And Jesus Said . . .   242

Lesson 33   To Do as He Did   248

Lesson 34   The Promise   256

Acknowledgments

Always there was God. Always there will be God. Through studying His Word and the lives of His servants, you will learn and grow as you become like Him.

unit 1

WHO IS GOD?

While You're Studying
WHO IS GOD?

A Begin a memory verse file for the year. This file can be in the form of a journal, cards, inexpensive photo album, computer program, etc. Each week add the memory verse to your file.

B Create an acrostic using the words *Living Water* or *Bread of Life* to tell the attributes of these gifts.

C Make a mobile or create a word wall using adjectives that describe the Members of the Godhead.

D As a culminating activity for the unit, publish a newspaper covering the topics that were studied. Your paper could include feature articles about each of the lessons, artwork, an advice column, letters to the editor, photos, an editorial, or poetry.

© DARREL TANK

WHO IS GOD?

Memory Verse

"I have hidden your word in my heart, that I might not sin against you" (Psalm 119:11).

Living Water, what is it? Bread of Life? Never hunger again? What does Jesus offer those who ask, who search?

An Ancient Book Written for You

John 4:1–42

For thousands of years the Bible has given courage and help to all kinds of people in all kinds of places. This ancient Book had an up-to-date message for Jim and Bob and their friends who were prisoners of war. James Ray, a captain in the United States Air Force, tells this story:

Psst. It sounded like a whisper. I struggled to sit up in my solitary cell, trying to hear, but I must have been dreaming. I slumped back, wondering how long it had been since my plane had been shot down. I tried to forget the weeks since my capture, the endless questioning, the torture, and the helplessness.

Psst. Again the whisper. "Hey, Buddy!" The words came from the next cell. I flattened myself on the floor and peered through the crack under the door. "I'm Bob Purcell, U.S. Air Force," a voice whispered. We waited as a guard passed and then began whispering again.

I learned that there were some other Americans in the prison. Soon all of us were secretly whispering. We started by learning about one another, where we were from, our families, the war, wondering if we would ever be free again.

One day Bob asked, "Do you know any Bible verses?"

"Well, the Lord's Prayer," I answered.

"How about the twenty-third psalm?"

"Only a little of it."

I began whispering what I could remember, and he'd repeat each phrase after me.

Other prisoners joined in, sharing verses they knew. Through the sessions a fellowship grew among us. And how we needed it! We spent twenty hours a day locked in our cells. Our diet of rice and thin soup made from pumpkin and cabbage left us hungry, weak, and sick. Those Bible verses became a constant assurance to us of God's love and care.

When do you think these men learned these Bible verses?

WHO IS GOD?

As the days dragged on, we were able to share a great deal of Scripture.

We made ink from brick dust and water or drops of medicine. We'd write verses on bits of toilet paper and pass them around, even though communication was forbidden. A man caught passing a note would be forced to stand for hours with his arms up against a wall with no chance to sleep.

But the urge to share those marvelous words of comfort was stronger than our fear of punishment. One night I lay with my ear pressed against the wall of my cell and heard *tap . . . tap . . . tap.* From somewhere a fellow prisoner of war was tapping in Morse code: "I will lift up mine eyes unto the hills, from whence cometh my help" (Psalm 121:1, KJV).

He tapped out the rest of the psalm, which I scratched on the concrete floor with a piece of broken tile. "My help cometh from the LORD, which made heaven and earth," the psalm assured us. These words brought comfort and hope to us.

Two and a half years went by before I could write to Dad and Mother. A year later I was allowed to receive my first letter. In the meantime, we lived on letters written over two thousand years ago.

What would you like to have "stored" in your mind if you were in isolation for a long period of time?

Finally, after many requests, we were permitted to have a Bible for one hour each week. One of us was allowed to copy from it. But when we'd start, the guard would plant his elbow on the Bible for the first fifteen minutes. Then, after he'd let us start, he'd ask questions to try to distract us. We'd just ignore him and write as fast as we could.

The next week we'd have to return the portion we'd copied the previous week. Our captors seemed to be afraid to let us keep the scripture. It was as if they sensed that spiritual help kept us from losing our minds.

After five weeks, we didn't see the Bible again. But that had been enough time for us to memorize the Sermon on the Mount, Romans 12, 1 Corinthians 13, and many of the psalms. Now we had our own "living Bible." From this experience we learned a most important lesson. Bible verses on paper aren't nearly as useful as verses stored in your mind, where you can draw on them at any time for guidance and comfort.

What would you have written if you had a Bible for only one hour per week?

Years passed—years of sickness, endless hunger, and loneliness. We never knew if we'd ever see home again. But instead of going mad, we were able to sustain one another in compassion and understanding.

We were living proof of one of the verses I heard tapped out on the prison wall: "'People do not live by bread alone, but by every word that comes from the mouth of God'" (Matthew 4:4).*

What do you think these men had done before they were captured to make it possible for them to become "living Bibles"?

Life became worth living for those men as they placed their faith and future in the hands of One who gave "spiritual food," for it renewed their strength to meet their greatest needs.

How can spiritual food strengthen your faith?

Once when Jesus was talking to a great crowd of people, He gave a special promise to anyone who is "hungry" for spiritual food. "God blesses those who hunger and thirst for justice," He said, "for they will be satisfied" (Matthew 5:6). Later, He explained, "I am the bread of life. Whoever comes to me will never be hungry again. Whoever believes in me will never be thirsty" (John 6:35).

What is promised to anyone who "hungers and thirsts for justice?"

Another time Jesus asked a stranger for a drink of water, but she wasn't sure she should give it to Him. The Bible tells the story this way:

"Soon a Samaritan woman came to draw water. Jesus said to her, 'Please give me a drink.' He was alone at the time because His disciples had gone into the village to buy some food.

"The woman was surprised, for Jews refused to have anything to do with Samaritans. She said to Jesus, 'You are a Jew, and I am a Samaritan woman. Why are you asking me for a drink?'

"Jesus replied, 'If you only knew the gift God has for you and who you are speaking to, you would ask me, and I would give you living water.'

"'But sir, you don't have a rope or a bucket,' she said, 'and this well is very deep. Where would you get this living water? And besides, do you think you're greater than our ancestor Jacob who gave us this well? How can you offer better

WHO IS GOD?

water than he and his sons and his cattle enjoyed?'

"Jesus replied, 'Anyone who drinks this water will soon become thirsty again. But those who drink the water I give will never be thirsty again. It becomes a fresh, bubbling spring within them, giving them eternal life'" (John 4:7–14).

The bread of life, living water. These are word pictures Jesus used to help you

understand what He can do for you. His words are like good food to anyone who is "hungry" to listen to them. His words are like sparkling cold water for people who are "thirsty" to know more about Him.

Nothing will strengthen your mind more than thoughtful reading of the Bible. You cannot depend on what someone else has read for the spiritual "food" and "water." The personal, private time you spend with the Bible is the only way you can gain the value of His Word. Only by letting it infiltrate your life can you be assured of positive results. "By beholding Christ, you will become changed. . . . You will practice love, patience, gentleness, goodness, mercy, and every grace that dwells in the child of God, and will at last find a place among the sanctified and holy"(*Selected Messages*, bk. 1, p. 388). Angels from heaven will be with you, guiding your thoughts.

Through your study of the Bible this year, you will have opportunity to discover answers to these questions:

Who is God?

What is He like?

Can I know Him? How?

The Bible can give you courage and hope. It can give you confidence and security, just as it did for Jim and Bob and all their fellow prisoners. It can be the bread of life and living water, a gift from God to you.

*Adapted from *Guideposts*, July 1973.

WHO IS GOD?

Journal

- Write about a time when Scripture has been of comfort to you.

Dig a Little Deeper

1. What promise in each text would give comfort to men in prison?
   Romans 8:38, 39
   John 14:1–3
   Nahum 1:7
   Isaiah 41:10

2. Explain what you think Jesus meant when He said that He is the "bread of life" and the "living water." Read John 6:35, 63; 4:14; Isaiah 55:10; Matthew 4:4.

3. Why is memorization valuable to the learner?

4. Why is the reference to Jesus being the Bread of Life and the Living Water appropriate to the growth of an individual?

Activities

A. Imagine circumstances in which you would like to recall the Bible texts you have committed to memory. In small groups, compile a list of verses you know. Then, as a class, share the verses you recall. List verses you would like to add to your memory banks.

B. The words of God are illustrated by many figures of speech in the Bible. Find these symbols or figures of speech in the following texts. The first one is done for you. After completing the list, use these symbols to make a collage or mobile representing the Word of God.
    Ephesians 6:13, 17: armor, helmet, sword
    Psalm 119:105
    Mark 4:14
    John 4:7–14
    John 6:35
    Matthew 13:22, 23
    Hebrews 4:12

C. Using texts from your lesson and others you may research in a Bible concordance or dictionary, design a restaurant menu from which you order a spiritual dinner.

D. Construct a muslin wall hanging of a favorite Bible verse or poem. Draw your design on the fabric and color it with wax crayons. Place the fabric between two sheets of paper and then iron it with a warm iron to melt the color into the fabric.

To Learn More

The Bible Story, vol. 7, pp. 145–150
The Bible Pageant (1986), vol. 1, pp. 9–13

2

WHO IS GOD?

Memory Verse

Memory Verse

"The word of the LORD holds true, and we can trust everything he does"
(Psalm 33:4).

A Coptic translation of Paul's letter to the
Colossians written on papyrus, circa 275 A.D.

**How can we know what the Bible says is true? We know it is not
just an ordinary book because it was given to us by God, and He has
protected and preserved it through century after century. How and
under what circumstances was the Bible written?**

God's Word in Human Languages

2 Peter 1:12–21

The Bible is no ordinary book. Neither is it a new one. It did not suddenly appear as you see it now, all finished and neatly bound. Making it took not just years, but centuries.

It was written by people who lived in different generations and in different countries and who wrote in different languages. You might call it a library under one cover, for the Bible is a collection of sixty-six books and letters. The first thirty-nine books, known as the Old Testament, were written over a period of about eleven hundred years. The oldest books were ancient when Jesus came to live on earth. The last twenty-seven books, known as the New Testament, were written in only sixty years. The last book was written in approximately A.D. 100. Four hundred years elapsed between the writing of the Old and New Testaments.

Another name for the Bible is the Word of God. Although God did not write it Himself, He did choose people whom He could trust to write it for Him. They were God's friends. They knew Him so well that they recognized His message. Moses was one of those people. "Inside the Tent of Meeting, the LORD would speak to Moses face to face, as one speaks to a friend" (Exodus 33:11).

The writers included a shepherd, a king, an exiled priest, an advisor to an idol-worshiping king, a fruit picker, a tax collector, a physician, a "minister," the wisest man who ever lived, and at least two fishermen.

How could these men who were so different, and who wrote about different things in different times and different places, write *one* book? The Bible itself gives us the answer: "Above all, you must realize that no prophecy in Scripture ever came from the prophet's own understanding, or from human initiative. No, those prophets were moved by the Holy Spirit, and they spoke from God" (2 Peter 1:20, 21).

God guided the men to whom He gave His messages. Although the words

WHO IS GOD?

they used were their own, God directed their minds so that the messages were just what He wanted people to understand.

The original books or letters were all written by hand long before printing presses had been invented. Some parts of the Bible were written on animal skins that had been specially prepared, some on a type of paper called papyrus, some on clay tablets, and others on stone. Some of the "pens" used by the writers probably were made of feathers with the quills whittled down to a fine point. Others were a kind of chisel or stylus. Not a single one of the original books or letters still exists today.

Centuries before Christ, men who had great respect and reverence for those writings from God began to copy them. Few people could read or write, so these copiers, called scribes, were important people. Down through the centuries, one scribe after another copied and recopied the sacred messages, all by hand. Hundreds of years before Christ came to earth, men had copied the entire Old Testament, which they called "The Law and the Prophets." Jesus read those ancient writings and often mentioned them as He talked with the people who gathered to listen to Him. Picture Jesus reading the same Old Testament stories and messages in His language that you are able to read in yours today!

About a thousand years ago, a group of Jewish scribes called Masoretes (MAZ-uh-reets) made a set of rules to be used in copying the ancient manuscripts. These rules helped to preserve the accuracy of the copies they were making. These men had such respect for God's Word that they did not want to make a single mistake. They knew exactly how many words and letters were in the entire Old Testament. They even knew how many times each letter appeared in the original manuscript. They would not write one letter or word from memory. The scribe looked at each word and said it out loud before he wrote it down.

What precautions were taken so that mistakes in copying were not made?

The rules did not permit a scribe to erase. If even one letter needed to be changed, the entire copy had to be thrown away and a new one begun. Any mistake, no matter how small, must not be corrected. The manuscript had to be destroyed.

The work of the Masorete scribes was much more difficult than such a task would be today, for in those days there were no chapters or verses, no punctuation, and no spaces between words. Some of the manuscripts did not even have vowels. Suppose you were the scribe and you came to this sentence:

NTHBGNNNGGDCRTDTHHVNSNDTHRTH

Could you read it? (If you have trouble, try reading Genesis 1:1.)

Not all of the manuscripts were copied as carefully as those made by the Masoretes, so not all of them are exactly alike. However, Bible scholars who compare many different manuscripts assure us that the differences are so minor that we can have absolute faith in the accuracy of the Bible.

The entire Old Testament was eventually translated from the ancient language in which it was first written, into Greek. Greek was also the language used in writing the New Testament some years after Jesus returned to heaven. Little by little the entire Bible was also translated into Latin.

In the year 1380, an Englishman named John Wycliffe and a group of his friends began to translate the Bible from Latin into English. What a task! They had to read the Latin words, then decide what each one meant and what English word to use in its place. When that was done, they had to write the English words by hand. It was difficult, slow work.

It was dangerous work too. People of great authority in England did not want the Bible translated into a language that everyone could read. Church leaders said that ordinary people would not be able to understand it. In reality, they did not want people to understand the Bible. These leaders wanted people to depend on what was told them, rather than on reading the Word of God for themselves. The church was so powerful that it made laws governing the way people were to worship. Anyone who disobeyed these laws risked severe punishment, and perhaps death.

Why was it dangerous work to translate the Bible into English?

People were taught that the only way they could talk to God or be forgiven for their sins was through the church. They were taught that only men who worked for the church could interpret the Bible. Since the Bible was written in Latin, most people had no way of knowing whether what the leaders taught them was true.

In spite of the danger, Wycliffe was determined that English-speaking people should be able to read the Bible for themselves.

Why did John Wycliffe and his friends decide to translate the Bible into English?

WHO IS GOD?

His huge task was finished in 1382, more than one hundred years before Columbus came to America. Can you imagine Wycliffe's joy when the last word was written? It was the very first English translation of the complete Bible. However, only wealthy people could afford the expensive, handwritten copies.

About one hundred fifty years later, a young man named William Tyndale took the next step in making the Bible available for English-speaking people. Only a few copies of Wycliffe's Bible had been made. Besides, they were difficult to read. William Tyndale was determined to make a new translation. He would use such simple words that even a child could read it and understand.

How did William Tyndale's work differ from that of John Wycliffe?

He endured hardships, threats, and fierce opposition. Escaping from England as a fugitive, Tyndale was persecuted, thrown into prison, and finally killed. Just before he died, he prayed, "Lord, open the King of England's eyes."

Tyndale did not live to complete the task he had begun, but others did it for him. By the time the Bible was finished, Johannes Gutenberg, a printer who lived in Germany, had invented a way to print books in quantity. Soon thousands of Tyndale's Bibles were smuggled into England and bought by people all over the country. Wherever the story of how we got our Bible is told, the name of William Tyndale is remembered and honored.

Why is the name of Johannes Gutenberg so important in the story of how we got our Bible?

Years later, Tyndale's last prayer was answered in a marvelous way. James I, King of England, appointed fifty-four of the best scholars in the land to make a new translation based on the work of Wycliffe, Tyndale, and other Englishmen. They finished their work in 1611, shortly before the Pilgrims came to America. Their King James Version is still the most famous of all English translations.

From that time to this, dozens of new translations have been made. Perhaps you wonder why scholars bother to make new ones when we still have the famous King James Bible. There are good reasons for doing so. The King James Bible was clear and plain to the people who read it hundreds of years ago. However, many of its words sound strange to us. For example, *thee, thou, thy, wilt,* and *shouldst.* But the words *you, your, will,* and *should* would have sounded just as strange in 1611.

The meanings of many English words have changed too. Look at the differences between the way Philippians 4:14 was translated in 1611 and today.

King James Version: "Notwithstanding ye have well done, that ye did communicate with my affliction."

New Living Translation: "Even so, you have done well to share with me in my present difficulty."

Now look at Romans 8:19 as it appears in several different translations and decide which one is the easiest to read and understand.

King James Version: "The earnest expectation of the creature waiteth for the manifestation of the sons of God."

New International Version: "The creation waits in eager expectation for the sons of God to be revealed."

Today's English Version: "All of creation waits with eager longing for God to reveal his sons."

Phillips, revised edition: "The whole creation is on tiptoe to see the wonderful sight of the sons of God coming into their own."

New Living Translation: "All creation is waiting eagerly for that future day when God will reveal who His children really are."

There is an even more important reason for making new translations. Since the King James Version was published, archaeologists working in Palestine, Egypt, Lebanon, Syria, and other countries have found thousands of ancient manuscripts and other objects. These artifacts are priceless treasures. By studying them, scholars are able to discover the original meaning of certain words and phrases in the Bible that were not so clear before.

There are many stories of how these ancient manuscripts were preserved. Not everyone realized their value. One person who did was Count Konstantin von Tischendorf, a great Bible scholar and traveler who lived from 1815 to 1874.

Once when he was visiting an old monastery at the foot of Mount Sinai, he found a huge basket filled with torn sheets of parchment. He recognized the writing. These were pages from a very old Greek Bible, parts of the Old Testament that must have been copied more than fifteen hundred years earlier! He learned, to his horror, that some of the pages had already been burned. The men who lived in the monastery were suspicious of Count Tischendorf. At first they refused to let him have the precious pages. It took patience and time to rescue them, but he finally succeeded. He had the pages copied and published. They are called the Codex Sinaiticus (Sign-NIGH-ti-kihs), one of the most valuable biblical treasures ever found.

Tischendorf's discovery inspired other men to search the monasteries, caves, and even in the desert in the hope that they, too, could find such treasures. One group exploring in the Egyptian desert came upon an ancient cemetery. As they dug away the sand from the tombs, they were disappointed to find only mummies of crocodiles. A disgusted workman kicked at one of them, and, to his amazement, it split open. Out tumbled rolls and rolls of papyrus manuscripts! The rolls contained many kinds of records. There were letters, legal documents, even recipes. Best of all, among these things the explorers found fragments of Bible verses that had been hidden away inside the crocodile mummies for more than eighteen hundred years.

In the spring of 1947 another amazing discovery was made quite by accident. Some Bedouin* boys were herding goats on a mountainside not far from the Dead Sea. One day while idly tossing rocks into the mouth of a cave above them, they heard the sound of pottery breaking. Curious, they climbed up the rocks and peered into the cave. In the semidarkness they could see a number of clay jars. When they explored the cave, they found that most of the jars were empty, but a few were filled with rolls of something that looked like leather.

The Bedouins tried to sell the objects the boys had found. At first buyers of antiques were afraid the rolls were fakes. Finally, however, biblical scholars learned of the discovery and were able to buy them. Some of these Dead Sea Scrolls, as they are now called, are actually extremely old copies of portions of the Bible.

Archaeologists and other Bible scholars explored a large area around the cave and found hundreds of

Qumran Caves, where the Dead Sea Scrolls were found.

priceless scrolls, jars, fragments of manuscripts, and linen cloth. These great treasures, which are the earliest known Bible manuscripts, include almost all of the books of the Old Testament. The words are very much like those in the Scriptures that Jesus read when He lived in Palestine two thousand years ago. These Dead Sea Scrolls provide additional proof that the men who copied in those long-ago days worked accurately and faithfully to preserve God's Word.

Why was the discovery of the Dead Sea Scrolls so important?

Through the centuries since Moses wrote the first books of the Bible, God has watched over His Word:

Protecting it when it was written by hand.

Protecting it when it was being translated into different languages.

Protecting it from wicked men who tried desperately to destroy it.

Protecting it for you.

You can read it and believe it.

You can trust the Bible!

* Tribes of people who wander through Arabian, Syrian, and North African deserts with no permanent home.

WHO IS GOD?

Journal

- Select one or two of your favorite Bible texts and explain why they are important to you.

Dig a Little Deeper

1. The Bible is often called the Word of God. With whom does it begin? Genesis 1:1. With whom does it end? Revelation 22:21.

2. Why do we call the Bible the Word of God if God did not dictate the actual words in it? 2 Peter 1:21

3. Name at least three ways God communicated with Bible writers. Numbers 12:6; Revelation 1:9–11; Daniel 9:21, 22

4. God chose people from a variety of occupations to be the writers of the Bible. Match the prophet-writer with the correct occupation from the following lists:

Ezra 7:12	Ezra	Ruler
Nehemiah 1:11	Nehemiah	Shepherd, fruit picker
Ezekiel 1:3	Ezekiel	Scribe, priest
Daniel 2:48	Daniel	Priest
Amos 7:14	Amos	King's cupbearer

5. Give at least two reasons why new translations of the Bible continue to be made.

6. Read the following four translations of James 1:2 and respond to the questions below.
   - King James Version: "My brethen, count it all joy when ye fall into divers temptations."
   - Today's English Version: "My brothers, consider yourselves fortunate when all kinds of trials come your way."
   - New International Version: "Consider it pure joy, my brothers, whenever you face trials of many kinds."
   - New Living Translation: "Dear brothers and sisters, when troubles come your way, consider it an opportunity for great joy."
   a. Which one is the easiest for you to read? Why?
   b. The word *divers* in the KJV text has changed in usage over the years. By comparing the text in the KJV with the other versions, what do you think *divers* means? Check with a dictionary to see if you are correct.
   c. Have the new translations changed the meaning of this text? Explain.

7. Below are a few verses that can help you meet a problem you may be having, an emergency, or a special need. Summarize each verse.
   - When you feel weak and helpless: Philippians 4:13
   - When you are in danger: Psalm 34:7, 8
   - When you are afraid: Psalm 56:3, 4
   - When you are tired, depressed, or worried: Matthew 11:28–30

Activities

A. Make a clay tablet. Write a Bible verse on it using something other than a modern writing tool.

B. Look up your memory verse in at least four different translations of the Bible and decide which is the easiest for you to understand. Make a poster that includes the verse and decorate it.
   OR
   Write it in the form used by the Masorete scribes. Make a poster with the verse and decorate it.

C. Choose one of the following topics for further study and prepare a report to give to the class or present as an interview for your class. Work with a classmate.
   1. Incidents from the life of William Tyndale, Miles Coverdale, or John Wycliffe.
   2. The discovery, value, and translation of the Dead Sea Scrolls or the Codex Sinaiticus.
   3. The story of Johannes Gutenberg and his great invention.

D. Make a timeline of yarn that illustrates the approximate periods of history covered by the Bible. Create a ratio that will allow you to use one wall or the perimeter of your classroom. Include the following:
   Creation to Flood = 2,000 years (blue yarn)
   Flood to Moses = 1,000 years (green yarn)
   Moses to Christ = 1,500 years (yellow yarn)
   Christ's life = 33 years (red yarn)
   Christ to present = 2,000 years (white yarn)

To Learn More

The Bible Pageant (1986), vol. 1, pp. 14–23
God's Smuggler by Brother Andrew (Grand Rapids, Mich.: Chosen Books, 2001)
For an excellent account of how we got our Bible, see a condensation of the book *Miracle of the Book* by Ruth Wheeler and Eugene W. Erickson included in the *SDA Advanced Reading Program* (Pacific Press® Publishing Association, 1972), bk. 3, pp. 640–759

3

WHO IS GOD?

Memory Verse

"May the grace of our Lord Jesus Christ, the love of God, and the fellowship of the Holy Spirit be with you all" (2 Corinthians 13:14).

There are some realities the human mind cannot understand— long periods of time, speed, great distance, the heat of the sun, the size of the galaxy, eternity. We get glimpses of meaning, we understand in a limited sense, but we cannot really comprehend many realities in our universe. Nevertheless, we accept by faith the size of the galaxy, the speed of light, the temperature of the sun. Because we cannot fully understand God, we must accept by faith His eternal existence and His nature. The Bible tells us as much as we can comprehend about God. From the study of the Bible, what do we know about the nature of God?

Always There Is God

John 1

> Before the World was
> > there was God.
> Before the stars, the moon, the sun,
> > there was God.
> Before the angels,
> > there was God.
> Always, there IS God.

Back in time, back before history—back before there was a world or a sun, a moon or a star, or any created being, there was God.

The Bible tells us that God is eternal. "From beginning to end, you are God" (Psalm 90:2). There never was a time without God. There never will be. Everything on this planet has a beginning and an ending, but God had no beginning, and He will never come to an end. Although we cannot understand this mystery, we can believe that God is Someone who loves us infinitely. He was present before our world began, and He was present when our world was created. Throughout history He has been there, revealing His love to us.

God is eternal. What does eternal mean?

In the Old Testament, God is identified by the name *Yahweh* (which is often translated as "the LORD" in English versions of the Bible, and which is the source of the English word *Jehovah).* The meaning of *Yahweh* is similar to "eternal." If someone were to ask, "Who is the God of the Hebrews?" the answer would be, "Yahweh, the eternal." The Israelites held this name to be so sacred that they did not speak it aloud.

What is the Hebrew name of the God of the Bible?

In the New Testament, the same God is identified by a different name. It is not just one word (like Yahweh), but a group of words together, giving us a new name for God: Father, Son, and Holy Spirit. We don't often think of these words as the Christian name of God, but that is really what they are. If someone were to ask, "Who is the God of the Christians?" the proper answer would be, "The God who is the Father, Son, and Holy Spirit."

It is difficult for us to wrap our minds around the concept of one God in three separate Beings. The names used for each Member of the Godhead help us to understand the work that Each performs. The Christian name for God was used by Jesus when He directed His disciples. "Go and make disciples . . . baptizing them in the name of the Father and the Son and the Holy Spirit" (Matthew 28:19). It was used also by Paul in a familiar benediction that requests, "May the grace of our Lord Jesus Christ, the love of God, and the fellowship of the Holy Spirit be with you all" (2 Corinthians 13:14).

Just as it is difficult to understand how God has always existed and will always exist, so it is also difficult to understand the role and work of God the Father. God is just that: a Father, a loving Father, our Father. Ellen White describes Him in the book *The Desire of Ages*. "Satan has represented God as selfish, as oppressive, as claiming all, and giving nothing, as requiring the service of His creatures for His own glory, and making no sacrifice for their good. But the gift of Christ reveals the Father's heart. It testifies that the thoughts of God toward us are 'thoughts of peace, and not of evil.' Jeremiah 29:11. It declares that while God's hatred of sin is as strong as death, His love for the sinner is stronger than death" (p. 57).

Our Father, God, is described in Matthew 7:9–11. Jesus, talking to the people in what we refer to as the Sermon on the Mount, says this about God: "You parents—if your children ask for a loaf of bread, do you give them a stone instead? Or if they ask for a fish, do you give them a snake? Of course not! So if you sinful people know how to give good gifts to your children, how much more will your heavenly Father give good gifts to those who ask him." Luke quotes Jesus in much the same way in Luke 11:11–13.

A loving Father who loves to give His children good things—that is God. When we refer to God as "the Father," we mean He is the Father of the "only Son" (John 3:16), and He is the Father of all humanity. We are His sons and daughters. The most loving gift God could give was His Son, Jesus. Rather than convince God to love and save us, the gift of Jesus reveals His love and saving nature to us.

God shows love to us, and this loving Father wishes to have us reach out to the world with the holiness, the compassion, and giving nature that are His character. He loves us and in return gives us the opportunity to love those around us (*The Desire of Ages*, pp. 677, 678). He works in us, through us, with us to develop characters reflecting His love. Then He shines through us to reveal this love to others.

How can we know God? How is God with us? God is not far away from us, somewhere off in heaven; He is here with us. God is not far away, somewhere back in history; He is present now. God is not far from us spiritually, as an observer of our lives; He is actively involved through the person of the Holy Spirit. The Spirit not only shows us the character of God but also invites us to make Him the Lord of our lives.

If Christ was the only Member of the Godhead to die, how was salvation a gift of all Three?

Although the external existence of God and the relationship of the Members of the Trinity are beyond our comprehension, we can know God. We can learn about Him as we study the Bible, His letter to us. He sent His Son to earth as a man. He has revealed Himself in ways we can understand. We can speak to Him when we pray, and we can experience God when the Holy Spirit is active in our lives. There may be things about God we do not understand, but we can know what He is like. We can invite Him into our lives.

We can know Him as our Friend and loving Father.

In what ways do we come to know God?

WHO IS GOD?

Journal

• Write a description of God, the loving Father.

Dig a Little Deeper

1. Who are the Three Members of the Trinity, or Godhead?

2. All Three Members of the Godhead were present at the baptism of Jesus. What did each One do at this event? Matthew 3:16, 17

3. To whom did Jesus tell us to pray? To whom does the word *your* refer? Matthew 6:6–9

4. What did Jesus say about
   a. The Father and forgiveness? Matthew 6:14, 15
   b. Your need to worry? Matthew 6:25–27
   c. Fear? Luke 12:32

5. What did God the Father say about Jesus? Mark 1:11; Matthew 17:1–5

6. What did Jesus say about the Holy Spirit? John 14:16, 17

7 Which Member of the Trinity is mentioned in both the first and last verse of the New Testament?

8. What does each of the following texts tell us about God?
   a. Genesis 1:1
   b. Malachi 3:6
   c. Isaiah 46:9, 10
   d. Jeremiah 23:24
   e. Psalm 147:5
   f. Psalm 103:8

9. When you think about God the Father, which of His characteristics do you think of first? Why?

Activities

A.   Choose a method to describe each Member of the Godhead. You might use three verses of a poem, three pictures, three symbols, or three prose descriptions.

B   After reading the following passages describing the Father, identify a problem a middle-school age student might experience, and tell how you believe God could be involved in the solution.

> "God is bending from His throne to hear the cry of the oppressed. To every sincere prayer He answers, 'Here am I.' He uplifts the distressed and downtrodden. In all our afflictions He is afflicted. In every temptation and every trial the angel of His presence is near to deliver" (*The Desire of Ages*, p. 356).

> "Satan works to fill people's hearts with doubt. He tempts them to sin, and then to consider themselves too wicked to approach their heavenly Father. But God understands all this. Jesus assured His disciples that every sigh of discouragement, every stab of pain, every wave of grief we feel is echoed in the heart of God" (*Messiah*, p. 210).

C.   Refer back to the scenario you described in Activity B. Write a letter to the person, sharing how God is willing to help them through this problem.

D.   Use a concordance to look up names for God the Father. Make a poster with the names and symbols.

To Learn More

Colossians 1:15–20
Mark 1:9–11
John 1:1–3
Messiah, chaps. 5; 37; 73

WHO IS GOD?

Memory Verse

"Jesus told him, 'I am the way, the truth, and the life. No one can come to the Father except through me. If you had really known me, you would know who my Father is. From now on, you do know him and have seen him!'" (John 14:6, 7).

In the previous lesson you studied about the Godhead—the Father, the Son, and the Holy Spirit. This lesson focuses on the Son, Jesus, who lived on earth. As you read about Jesus, you will also learn about God the Father. What can you learn about the Father by studying the life of Jesus?

"If You Have Seen Me . . ."

John 14; 15

I f you were asked to write everything you know about each Member of the Godhead, no doubt the list for the Son would be the longest. Perhaps your list about the Father would be the shortest. In the New Testament, God the Father's words are recorded on only three occasions: at Jesus' baptism, in the temple, and on the mount of transfiguration (Matthew 3:16, 17; 17:1–5; John 12:20–28). Each time He is speaking of the Son, Jesus. Because we know so much more about the Son than about the Father, it is important to understand that the Father is just like the Son.

Near the end of Jesus' life on earth, one of the disciples asked Him to show them the Father. Jesus told them, "'Anyone who has seen me has seen the Father!'" (John 14:9). "'The Father and I are one'" (John 10:30). In the book of Hebrews, Paul wrote that Christ "expresses the very character of God" (Hebrews 1:3). The Father and the Son are the same in character, in purpose, and in power. The best way to learn about both the Father and the Son is to study the life of Jesus on earth as recorded in the Bible. As we closely examine Jesus' life, we find many outstanding characteristics.

What does "expresses the very character of God" mean?

Jesus is kind. Some examples of His kindness included saving a bridegroom from embarrassment because the wine ran out at his wedding feast and raising from the dead the only son of a widow from the town of Nain. Children recognized Jesus' kindness and wanted to be with Him. When Jesus' disciples tried to send children away, Jesus stopped the disciples and gave the children a special invitation to come to Him. The sick also came in great numbers to be healed;

even lepers came when they heard that Jesus could cure them.

Jesus is concerned about everyone. In fact, Jesus was criticized because of His concern for the poor, the tax collectors, the foreigners, and the sinners. Religious leaders, important people, and even His own disciples could not understand Him. It puzzled the disciples that Jesus would go home with Zacchaeus to eat and that He would call Levi Matthew, a tax collector, to be a disciple. They were surprised that He would talk publicly with a woman—especially one from Samaria, and heal the daughter of a foreign woman. Jesus healed the servant of a Roman officer, even though the Romans and Jews hated each other. The Pharisees were outraged that Jesus ate with sinners and that He forgave a woman caught in adultery. The Jews believed that riches were a gift from God to the righteous, but Jesus said it was easier for a camel to pass through the eye of the needle than for a rich man to be saved. Jesus' concern for everyone—the poor, foreigners, and sinners—was incomprehensible to both His friends and enemies.

Why do you think Jesus broke the custom of the day by associating with and helping these people?

Jesus is patient. Nowhere is this more clearly demonstrated than in Jesus' treatment of His disciples. Jesus' disciples lived with Him for three years, watching Him perform miracles, listening to His preaching, and receiving direct instruction. But they were slow to understand His teachings or mission. They were still fighting over who would be the greatest in Christ's kingdom. The words of Jesus about serving others, putting others first, and denying one's self seemed lost on them. The night before His crucifixion, Christ washed the disciples' feet Himself, because each disciple was waiting for one of the others to do it. In spite of their failings, Jesus loved them and patiently worked with them. After His resurrection, eleven of the twelve disciples became the leaders of the early church.

Jesus is firm. Although Jesus demonstrated patience, love, and understanding, He did not tolerate hypocrisy, irreverence, and self-righteousness. Twice He drove the money changers with their animals out of the temple. These men cheated the people and used God's house to make money for themselves. The Pharisees, who were so proud of their righteousness, were sternly rebuked for hypocrisy. One time Jesus called them a "brood of snakes" (Matthew 12:34) and on another occasion "whitewashed tombs" (Matthew 23:27). Even Christ's disciples were sometimes rebuked. When Peter contradicted Jesus, Christ responded with the words, "Get away from me, Satan!" (Matthew 16:23). Some people thought God would overlook their wrong actions because of His patience and kindness. Jesus made it clear that sin is offensive to God.

> ### *Why did Jesus use the terms "brood of snakes" and "whitewashed tombs" to describe the Pharisees?*

Jesus is forgiving. Throughout His life on earth, Jesus forgave those who were considered by some to be unforgivable. The Pharisees became very angry when He said, "Your sins are forgiven" (Matthew 9:2), to a paralyzed man whose friends lowered him through a hole in the roof of a house. The Pharisees did not accept Jesus as the Messiah, so they did not believe that He could forgive sin.

The greatest demonstration of Jesus' love and forgiveness was at the time of His crucifixion. Although exhausted, in great pain, and facing the ordeal of dying, Jesus' thoughts were for others. He forgave the thief on the cross beside Him when he asked for forgiveness. He also prayed for those who did not ask. As the soldiers nailed Him to the cross, Jesus prayed, "Father, forgive them, for they don't know what they are doing" (Luke 23:34).

> ### *What were the greatest demonstrations of Jesus' love and forgiveness?*

Jesus is our Creator and our Redeemer. He came to earth not only to die for our sins but also to live among us that we might know Him. As we come to know more about Jesus, we come to know more about the Father also. When Satan started sin in heaven, he accused God of being cruel, unjust, and impossible to please. As we study the life of Jesus, we see for ourselves that Satan lied.

WHO IS GOD?

Journal

- Imagine that you spent a day with Jesus. Write about how you may have felt as you watched Jesus' reactions to both His friends and enemies.

Dig a Little Deeper

1. In John 14:1–10 a promise is recorded.
   a. What promise did Jesus make to the disciples?
   b. What did Jesus say the disciples knew?
   c. What question did Thomas ask Jesus? How did Jesus respond?
   d. What request did Philip make of Jesus? What was Jesus' response?
   e. What do you think Jesus wanted His disciples to understand?

2. Paul talks about the Father's relationship to the Son. List three things that tell us about this relationship. Hebrews 1:1–3

3. Choose one of the characteristics of Jesus mentioned in this lesson and illustrate it with a Bible story that is not included in the lesson. Write the story in your own words.

4. Summarize the following texts. What attributes of Jesus are demonstrated in each?
   a. Matthew 9:1–8; Mark 2:1–5; Luke 5:17–26
   b. Matthew 15:32–39; Mark 8:1–10
   c. Matthew 10:1–15; Mark 6:7–13; Luke 9:1–6
   d. Luke 10:38–41
   e. John 9:1–34

What can you conclude about God the Father after studying these texts?

Activities

A. Write a short quiz covering today's lesson. Give it to your classmates and discuss the answers with them.

B. Look through the *Seventh-day Adventist Hymnal* to find at least three hymns about Jesus. Choose one and write an additional verse for it.

C. Select a story from the life of Jesus that you would like to illustrate. Create a "stained glass picture" using a piece of clear plastic and transparent paint or crayons. Mount your picture in a window so that the light can shine through the "stained glass." As an alternative, draw and color your picture on white paper; then oil it completely with baby or cooking oil.

D. Play a recording of "Unto Us a Child Is Born," chorus No. 12, Handel's *Messiah.* Find the text in Isaiah on which the chorus is based.

To Learn More

The Desire of Ages, chaps. 1; 8
Messiah, chaps. 1; 8
Patriarchs and Prophets, pp. 33–43, 52
Selected Messages, bk. 1, pp. 311–319
Steps to Christ, chaps. 1; 2
The Story of Redemption, pp. 13–51

WHO IS GOD?

Memory Verse

"The Holy Spirit produces this kind of fruit in our lives: love, joy, peace, patience, kindness, goodness, faithfulness, gentleness, and self-control. There is no law against these things!" (Galatians 5:22, 23).

The Father, the Son, and the Holy Spirit are always in perfect harmony. When God created our world, the Holy Spirit was there. All through the Old Testament days, the Holy Spirit was at work, guiding, helping, and protecting. When Jesus came to live on this earth, the Holy Spirit was with Him.

The Holy Spirit was the gift that Jesus promised to His disciples before He returned to His Father. That promise holds true for you today.

A Comforter Is Sent

John 15:26

In the moonlight, the road stretched like a silver ribbon, its edges bordered with trees and vines that twisted along the rocky fences. The eleven men walking with Jesus that Thursday evening were not thinking of the beauty of the soft spring night. They were puzzled and worried about what Jesus was telling them. "I will ask the Father, and he will give you another Advocate, who will never leave you. He is the Holy Spirit, who leads into all truth. The world cannot receive him, because it isn't looking for him and doesn't recognize him. But know him, because he lives with you now and later will be in you. No, I will not abandon you as orphans—I will come to you." "When the Father sends the Advocate as my representative—that is, the Holy Spirit—he will teach you everything and will remind you of everything I have told you" (John 14:16–18, 26). Jesus was promising the gift of the Holy Spirit, the Third Member of the Godhead.

After His resurrection, Jesus once again walked with His disciples. For forty days He spent much time with His followers. He talked with them about the kingdom of God. He told them what the Holy Spirit would do for them. He explained what their work on earth was to be. "Go and make disciples of all the nations, baptizing them in the name of the Father and the Son and the Holy Spirit. Teach these new disciples to obey all the commands I have given you. And be sure of this: I am with you always, even to the end of the age" (Matthew 28:19, 20).

Jesus explained that the Holy Spirit would now become their Teacher and their Counselor. He would help them remember what Jesus had taught them. He would give them the ability to explain to others about Jesus' death and resurrection.

What did Jesus tell His disciples that the Holy Spirit would help them do?

WHO IS GOD?

As they were eating together, He said, "Do not leave Jerusalem until the Father sends you the gift he promised, as I told you before." "You will receive power when the Holy Spirit comes upon you. And you will be my witnesses, telling people about me everywhere—in Jerusalem, throughout Judea, in Samaria, and to the ends of the earth" (Acts 1:4, 8).

The time had come for Jesus to return to His Father. "The disciples gathered about Him. Beams of light seemed to radiate from His countenance as He looked lovingly upon them. . . . Words of the deepest tenderness were the last that fell upon their ears from the lips of their Lord. With hands outstretched in blessing, and as if in assurance of His protecting care, He slowly ascended from among them" (*The Desire of Ages,* pp. 830, 831). He was taken up into heaven, and the people gazed in awe until a cloud hid Him from their sight. Jesus was gone. But His friends were no longer worried or afraid because Jesus had promised He would send Someone like Himself to be with them. They had learned that they could trust Him. At last they understood what Jesus had told them that night on the way to the Garden of Gethsemane.

Jesus' followers went back to Jerusalem. People who didn't know what had happened expected the disciples to look sad and defeated. Instead, they were joyful and courageous. They were not mourning over the death of their Master. They were rejoicing that He was alive.

The disciples were not idle while they waited in Jerusalem for the gift Jesus had promised. They reminded one another of the wonderful things Jesus had done and had taught them. They spent much of their time praying for strength and wisdom to help people understand that Jesus is Lord. They were determined to tell the good news to everyone who would listen.

Sometime later when the disciples were together, they heard a sudden sound of wind. Something that looked like tongues of fire appeared to rest on them. These were a symbol of the Holy Spirit. They represented the heavenly power He was giving to the disciples. The disciples recognized that this was the gift Jesus had told them to wait for. They believed the Holy Spirit would always be with them and would give them everything they needed for the difficult work ahead. The Bible says that they all were "filled with the Holy Spirit" (Acts 2:4).

What does being "filled with the Holy Spirit" mean?

From that day on, the disciples traveled everywhere, obeying Jesus' command to teach all nations and baptize those who believed.

Jesus once compared the Holy Spirit to the wind. We cannot see the wind, but we know what it does. We cannot see the Holy Spirit, but we know what He does. We know that He is always ready and eager to help us. Our part is to invite Him to be with us. We will become more like Jesus if we are willing to listen to the Holy Spirit's voice and follow the instruction He has given in the Bible.

When we invite the Holy Spirit to be with us, He will lead us to understand the Bible. He will show us what we are doing that is wrong. He will help us to realize our need to follow Christ to change us into His likeness. He, like Jesus, is a special person we can call on for help.

The Holy Spirit in us produces love, joy, peace, patience, kindness, goodness, faithfulness, gentleness, and self-control. These character traits help us to be successful on earth and prepare us for heaven. The Bible calls them the fruit of the Spirit.

Why do you think the metaphor "fruit of the Spirit" is used?

Perhaps you have thought the minute you do something wrong, the Holy Spirit leaves you. That is not true! The Holy Spirit does not give up easily. He persists in helping you.

Remember the stories you have read about the people of Israel? Think how rebellious and stubborn they often were during the years they wandered in the wilderness. Yet, during all those years, the Holy Spirit stayed with them, always trying to help, never giving up.

He is just the same today.

You cannot know everything about how the Holy Spirit works for you, but you can know the most important things. He is just as interested in you as He was in the people who lived in the Bible days.

"In sorrow and affliction, when the outlook seems dark and the future perplexing, and we feel helpless and alone, these are the times when, in answer to the prayer of faith, the Holy Spirit brings comfort to the heart" (The Acts of the Apostles, p. 51).

WHO IS GOD?

Journal

- The Holy Spirit reveals Himself to us in many ways. Tell about a time that you were glad that you listened to the Holy Spirit. How did the Holy Spirit reveal Himself to you?

Dig a Little Deeper

1. The Holy Spirit is mentioned in the very first part of the first book of the Bible. He is also mentioned in the last part of the last chapter of the last book of the Bible. What is said of Him in each of these references?

2. The day the Holy Spirit first came to the disciples is known as what day? Describe the events of that occasion. Acts 2:1–4

3. List the things you find in your lesson and in the following verses that tell what the Holy Spirit will do for you. John 16:7, 13; Ezekiel 36:27; Isaiah 11:2

4. The book of Acts tells what happened to the first "church" when its members were filled with the Holy Spirit. Read Acts 1 and 2; then answer these questions:
   a. What did the members do to receive the Holy Spirit?
   b. What did the members do after they received the Holy Spirit?
   c. What did people in the community think of these Spirit-filled followers of Jesus?

5. Someday you may be asked what you believe and why you believe it. In John 14:26, the Holy Spirit is promised to prepare you for that time. Read the text and write what the Holy Spirit will do for you.

Activities

A. Imagine that you are one of the disciples waiting in Jerusalem for the special sign or symbol by which you would know that the Holy Spirit was going to be with you as you tell the world about Jesus. Complete the following phrases:
   1. While we were waiting for Jesus' promise of the Holy Spirit to be fulfilled, I felt . . .
   2. When I first saw the little flames, I wondered . . .
   3. As soon as I realized what was happening, I thought . . .
   4. The most wonderful part of the whole experience is that . . .

B. Use a concordance to find other names or descriptions of the Holy Spirit. Choose a method to illustrate.

C. The Holy Spirit shows Himself in our lives through "fruit of the Spirit"— evidences of His transforming power. Make a three-dimensional display depicting examples of the fruits of the Spirit you feel are demonstrated in your classroom. Suggest ways you and your class could share these evidences of the Spirit with people outside of your classroom.

D. Compare and contrast the following eyewitness accounts of Christ's ascension: Matthew 28:16–20; Mark 16:15–20; Luke 24:44–52; John 21:24, 25; Acts 1:1–11. Why do you think there are differences?

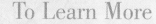

To Learn More

The Bible Story, vol. 9, pp. 151–155, 170–192; vol. 10, pp. 9–16
The Bible Pageant (1986), vol. 4, pp. 164–173; vol. 5, pp. 25–29
The Desire of Ages, chap. 73
Messiah, chap. 73
The Acts of the Apostles, pp. 47–56

Every one of us must decide whether we will serve God or Satan. When we decide to be on Christ's side, Jesus accepts us and immediately treats us as if we had never sinned. As Christians, we continue to become acquainted with the Savior; and our attitudes, goals, values, ideas, and feelings become more like His.

unit 2

CHANGING TO BECOME LIKE GOD

While You're Studying

A Write the memory verses for the unit and add them to your file.

B Create a bookmark that includes a Bible text on faith. Add illustrations and share your bookmark with someone if you wish.

C Make an ABC book of prayer. Illustrate each letter of the alphabet.

D As a culminating activity for the unit, publish a newspaper covering the topics that were studied. Your paper could include feature articles about each of the lessons, artwork, an advice column, letters to the editor, photos, an editorial, or poetry.

CHANGING TO BECOME LIKE GOD

Memory Verse

"Above all, you must realize that no prophecy in Scripture ever came from the prophet's own understanding, or from human initiative. No, those prophets were moved by the Holy Spirit, and they spoke from God" (2 Peter 1:20, 21).

God has many ways of communicating with people. He speaks through the beauty and grandeur of the world He created, He whispers through the still, small voice of the conscience, and He reveals Himself through human beings He chooses to speak for Him.

How does God choose people to speak for Him? How does He communicate through them?

They Spoke for God

Habakkuk 1–3; Zephaniah 1–3

From his watchtower high above the countryside of Judah, Habakkuk watched and waited. He had gone there to think about the amazing vision the Lord had given him and to listen for His voice again. Habakkuk did not have long to wait. "Write my answer plainly on tablets" (Habakkuk 2:2), said the Lord. In fact, Habakkuk was told to write so clearly that *everyone*, even people in a hurry, would see and read it. The revelation was a warning to the people of the land of Judah that a terrible crisis was coming. The heathen nation of Babylon was going to invade Judah and carry off thousands to be their slaves.

Why would God permit this to happen?

Almost all of His people had rejected Him. They had become rich by evil schemes. They had committed robbery and murder. They had gloated over the pain and grief they caused their victims. They worshiped idols that they themselves had made. These proud, wicked people had turned against God so completely that He could do nothing more for them.

Even in the midst of wickedness, a few people still trusted God and were distressed about the evil ways of their neighbors. Habakkuk, God's messenger, or prophet, was one of them. One of the messages God gave him was for these loyal men and women. Habakkuk told them that the stubborn pride of the wicked people of Judah would lead to the captivity of the whole nation. However, all those who trusted God would not need to be afraid, even in captivity. "The righteous will live by their faithfulness," God assured them (Habakkuk 2:4). He would never forsake them, for He was still in control of the affairs of earth.

We do not know anything at all about Habakkuk's family, but we do know that Habakkuk was a man whom God could trust as His messenger. He would be brave enough to tell the truth, no matter what happened.

What elements of Habakkuk's message would be relevant today?

CHANGING TO BECOME LIKE GOD

Zephaniah was another man God chose to speak for Him. In just one short paragraph in the Bible, Zephaniah gave a brief history about his family. He named his father, his grandfather, his great-grandfather, and his great-great-grandfather, a king named Hezekiah. Although Zephaniah was a member of a royal family, he didn't spend much time talking about himself. Like Habakkuk, Zephaniah had an important message from God for the people of Judah. Because of His great love, God had sent word to them again and again. However, they had made fun of His messengers. They "despised their words. They scoffed at the prophets" (2 Chronicles 36:16).

The people of Judah had turned away from the true God to worship false gods, some of which they made themselves. They were determined to have their own way no matter how it might hurt others. Almost all of them had become greedy, selfish cheats. But they were still God's people, and He loved them. In His great love for them, He sent a stern warning. Think of the courage it must have taken for Zephaniah to tell these wicked people that God was going to destroy the last traces of their idol worship. He also said God would punish those who were cheating, robbing, and killing innocent people.

? Why did it require courage for Zephaniah to deliver God's message?

But the message from God did not stop there. Zephaniah went on to give a message of comfort and hope to those who were willing to listen and obey God's instructions. God told Zephaniah to say,

"Be glad and rejoice with all your heart. . . !
Don't be afraid! For the LORD your God is living among you.
He is a mighty savior" (Zephaniah 3:14–17).

Of all the prophets to whom God spoke in Bible times, Haggai seemed to be the most successful in getting people to listen to him. The people of Judah had returned from captivity to find their homes and their temple in ruins. They were trying to rebuild the Lord's temple, but it was hard, dangerous work. Enemies were all around, constantly harassing them. The workers became so discouraged that they wanted to give up. They were anxious to rebuild their own homes. They made all kinds of excuses for stopping work on the temple. They seemed to forget the miraculous way in which God had brought them back to their own country. They acted as if they did not believe that God would be with them or protect them. They became more and more indifferent and neglectful, until at last all work on God's temple came to a standstill.

What are the risks associated with bearing witness for Christ today?

Just when it seemed things could not get worse, Haggai came to talk to these men and women of Judah. And what a difference he made! He reminded them of what the Lord had done for them. He reproved them for placing their own interests above their interest in God. He pointed out that the sight of the half-restored temple would make others think that God's people didn't think much of their God.

"Consider your ways," he begged his listeners. "Stop and think of your example to others. It doesn't look as if worshiping God is very important to you. Your own selfish interests seem to come first." He encouraged them to return to their task of completing work on the temple.

"Look at what's happening to you," he said.

And they did! Haggai's courageous message inspired people to act. As soon as they decided to honor God by completing His temple, Haggai's messages of reproof changed to words of encouragement from the Lord. " 'Be strong, all you people still left in the land. And now get to work, for I am with you, says the LORD of Heaven's Armies. My Spirit remains among you, just as I promised when you came out of Egypt. So do not be afraid' " (Haggai 2:4, 5).

The people went back to work on the temple. Their enemies were still around them, but the people of Judah put their trust in God. He honored their faith and protected them. They built so carefully and so well that the Lord declared, " 'I will fill this place with glory' " (Haggai 2:7).

How were the results of Haggai's work different from the two former prophets, Zephaniah and Habakkuk?

Habakkuk, Zephaniah, and Haggai were just three people in a long, long line of men and women whom God chose to be His messengers, or prophets. It was not the people themselves who decided they wanted to be prophets. God chose them and inspired them to speak for Him. Sometimes they made mistakes. Sometimes they were reluctant to take the responsibilities God gave them. None of them was perfect, but each listened to God. They did their

CHANGING TO BECOME LIKE GOD

best to deliver God's messages of instruction, warning, reproof, courage, hope, comfort, and assurance. Whenever there was a time of great need, God had a prophet who spoke for Him.

Peter, one of Jesus' disciples, explained it this way: "Those prophets were moved by the Holy Spirit, and they spoke from God" (2 Peter 1:21).

Habakkuk, Zephaniah, and Haggai are three of the prophets whose books have been preserved and are included in the Old Testament. There were other prophets (Miriam, Huldah, Elijah, and Elisha were some of them) who did not write any part of the Bible. John the Baptist was a prophet who lived in Jesus' day. Jesus called John the Baptist "the greatest of prophets," (*Testimonies*, vol. 5, p. 224), but John referred to himself as "a messenger" whose work was to announce the coming of Christ. He did not leave any written messages that have become part of the Bible.

The last book of the Bible, the book of Revelation, was written by John, the disciple of Jesus. He was the one whom Jesus first called a son of thunder, but who later became known as John the beloved. God gave John an outline of the history of our world and of the tremendous crisis to come. Although John could not understand everything, God told him to write what he saw. God would make the prophecies plain when the right time came. John called the special messages he was given "the testimony for [or about] Jesus" (Revelation 12:17) and the "eternal Good News" (Revelation 14:6).

Ever since those long-ago days, God has always had men and women whom He could trust to speak for Him. One of them was a girl named Ellen Harmon. God first spoke to her when she was a teenager. She was willing to listen and to obey God. For seventy years she studied and wrote and spoke for God just as did the prophets who lived in Bible days. It was estimated she received two thousand visions during her lifetime.

The messages that God gave Ellen White are of great importance to us, for they help us to know more about Him and His plans for us. Ellen White expressed the meaning of what God told her in the clearest way she possibly could. Her messages agree beautifully with the Bible. Again and again the counsel God gave her arrived at the right time and in just the right way to give instruction, warnings, courage, hope, and comfort, or to help solve a specific problem. The messages she recorded from God continue to prove true today.

Why are the messages given to Ellen White important to us?

Like John the Baptist, Ellen White often referred to herself as "a messenger." John gave his messages before Christ's first coming; Ellen White gave her messages before His second coming. Ellen White had no question that God had called her to speak for Him. One time she spoke of it in this way: "To claim to be a prophetess is something that I have never done. If others call me by that name, I have no controversy with them. But my work has covered so many lines that I cannot call myself other than a messenger, sent to bear a message from the Lord to His people, and to take up work in any line that He points out" (*Selected Messages,* bk. 1, p. 34).

You can read the messages God gave her in the books she wrote. You can trust the counsel and encouragement and information they contain. They are good news for you!

CHANGING TO BECOME LIKE GOD

Journal

- Describe how you might feel if God asked you to be a prophet.

Dig a Little Deeper

1. Habakkuk, Zephaniah, and Haggai were told to give to God's people a message containing both reproof/punishment and a promise. List the name of each prophet, the reproof/punishment, and the promise.

2. What qualifications of a true prophet can you find in the following references?
   a. Matthew 7:15–18
   b. Isaiah 8:20
   c. John 13:19
   d. 1 John 4:1, 2

3. In Ezekiel 40:2–4 the prophet Ezekiel describes a vision God gave him. He was told to do four things that explain the responsibility of any messenger for God. What are they?

4. The Bible contains the record of other people who claimed to be His messengers, but were not. What warning does God give us about such people? Matthew 24:23–26; Deuteronomy 13:1–3; 18:21, 22

5. Jude 14 and 15 identifies the first prophet. Who was he and what was his message?

6. Peter wrote that some of Paul's letters were hard to understand. Daniel could not understand the strange visions given him until God revealed their meanings. If those great men of Bible days had problems understanding parts of God's messages to His people, what about us?
   a. Does God hold us responsible for things we cannot understand? How does Deuteronomy 29:29 answer this question?
   b. Does this mean that we do not need to study the Bible? What is our responsibility?

Activities

A. Since Ellen White knew God so well and was blessed with special revelations from Him, she had some beautiful things to say about God and His plan for us. For example:

> "Take to Him everything that perplexes the mind. . . . Nothing that in any way concerns our peace is too small for Him to notice" (*Steps to Christ*, p. 100).

> "God never leads His children otherwise than they would choose to be led, if they could see the end from the beginning and discern the glory of the purpose which they are fulfilling as co-workers with Him" (*The Ministry of Healing*, p. 479).

Make a postcard using one of the above quotations or a Bible text or another quotation of your own choosing. On the front, write your quotation and decorate it attractively. On the reverse side write a personal message and mail it to someone who could use the encouragement.

B. Noah, Balaam, Jonah, and Peter also were prophets. God gave specific directions to each of them. Locate each prophet's story in your Bible and write what each was to do. Include the message they were to give and the people's response to their message.

C. Choose one of the prophets from the Bible and make an illustrated booklet of how God's plans were fulfilled. Choices may include: Miriam, Moses, Samuel, Elisha, Nathan, or Huldah.

D. First Kings 13:1–26 is an example of God's warnings against false prophets. Read the story; then tell it in your own words.

To Learn More

The Bible Story, vol. 6, pp. 92–95
Prophets Are People, Bobbie Jane Van Dolson (Review and Herald® Publishing Association, 1974)

CHANGING TO BECOME LIKE GOD

"Seek the LORD while you can find him. Call on him now while he is near. Let the wicked change their ways and banish the very thought of doing wrong. Let them turn to the LORD that he may have mercy on them. Yes, turn to our God, for he will forgive generously" (Isaiah 55:6, 7).

Sin is not a popular word. We don't want to be told that something we are doing is a sin. No one wants to be called a sinner. Even in our language, sin is played down. Words such as *naughty* or *troublesome* or *sick* are used. Although sin is the cause of so much trouble, it may often be laughed off as something only the preacher talks about.

But sin is important and deadly serious. It affects not only what happens to us for the rest of our lives on earth, but for eternity.

What is sin? Why is it more than something I do?

Sin Is More Than Something I Do

Romans 6:23

The sin problem started with Lucifer, the most intelligent, most powerful created being in the universe. When Lucifer became jealous of Christ and wanted to be God, he began a campaign of lies about God. As Lucifer's rebellion against his Creator spread among the other angels, he became Satan—the enemy of God.

Satan's lies continue today. He declares that God's laws are so unreasonable that no one can obey them. In fact, he insists that the only reason people even try to obey the law of God is that they are afraid of Him. Satan will do or say anything to try to separate us from God.

Many people think of sin only as the wrong things they do, such as being angry, hating someone, cheating, lying, bragging, or stealing. These things are sin, of course, but the sin problem lies deeper than that. The root is our self-centered nature that wants to be independent of God's control (Romans 8:6–8). The best-known biblical definition of sin is found in 1 John 3:4: "Everyone who sins is breaking God's law, for all sin is contrary to the law of God." Another version expresses the meaning in these words: "Everyone who sins breaks the law; in fact, sin is lawlessness" (NIV).

God's law is an expression of His will in two ways: physical law and moral law. The Creator placed all nature under physical or natural law. You may have discovered from your studies in science that everything in our world obeys the laws of nature. Intelligent beings—such as angels and the human family—are placed under the moral law as well.

Can you think of examples of God's natural and moral laws?

God's moral law is based on love: supreme love for the Creator and impartial love for other fellow beings. These principles are outlined in the Ten

CHANGING TO BECOME LIKE GOD

Commandments. The first four commandments define our love and duty to God; the last six define our love and duty to others. Moral law reflects the loving character of our Creator-God. It provides guidelines for the fullest happiness humans can enjoy.

Satan challenged God's moral law and questioned His motives for requiring obedience. He asserted his own independent will over God's will (Isaiah 14:12–14). He would obey none but himself. Many angels rebelled with him (Revelation 12:7–9). By leading Adam and Eve to disobey God, Satan started a rebellion on earth.

Why/how has everyone on the planet sinned?

Because Adam and Eve were the parents of the human race, their fall brought all humanity into a state of separation from God and rebellion against Him (Romans 8:6–8). With the exception of Jesus, everyone who has ever lived on this earth has sinned. We cannot, through our own efforts, change our sinful nature (Romans 3:23; Jeremiah 13:23). Adam and Eve's disobedience caused suffering and heartache for the Godhead and has caused endless trouble for the human family.

Some might question, "Why didn't God simply forgive Adam and Eve and let them have another chance?" This would seem to be the easy way, but perhaps these people do not understand the seriousness and the results of sin. Every nation has laws to enable its people to live together in peace and harmony. What do you suppose would happen if the judges and juries in our courts were to accept an "I am sorry" from every criminal and exact no penalty? In a short time our society and government would be in chaos. No government could survive that did not have consequences for the violation of its laws. So it is with the divine government. Justice is one aspect of good government. The honor of God's character and the stability of His government are involved. God would not be just if He simply excused sinners. The stability of the universe demands that God—its Sovereign—be just, as well as merciful.

In human society the seriousness of the crime determines the penalties for breaking the law. In God's government, however, the penalty for any sin is separation from God. Separation from God results in death (Romans 6:23). This may seem severe to us, but the self-centeredness of Satan's rule cannot coexist with God's rule of self-sacrificing love. Thus, God must—for the eternal good of the universe—ultimately destroy those beings who choose to remain in rebellion against Him.

The sin of Adam and Eve did not take God by surprise. In eternity—long before the creation of intelligent beings—the Trinity foresaw the emergence of sin and laid a plan to meet it. In Their great love for the human family, the Godhead moved to take the sin problem upon Themselves.

When was the plan made to help people who sinned against God?

"From the beginning, God and Christ knew of the apostasy of Satan, and of the fall of man through the deceptive power of the apostate. God did not ordain that sin should exist, but He foresaw its existence and made provision to meet the terrible emergency. So great was His love for the world, that He covenanted to give His only-begotten Son, 'that whosoever believeth in Him should not perish, but have everlasting life.' John 3:16" (*The Desire of Ages*, p. 22).

The plan the Godhead devised had two foundational pillars:

1. The *incarnation* of God the Son (John 1:1–3, 14; 1 Timothy 3:16).
2. The *substitutionary death* of God the Son (Hebrews 2:9).

The incarnation of God the Son is a mystery. The Son took upon Himself our human nature and was born of the virgin Mary (Luke 1:34, 35). He was named "Jesus" because He came to save the human family from sin (Matthew 1:21). Jesus was both fully divine and fully human. Jesus took our humanity for all eternity. He became the "Second Adam," the Head of the human race (Romans 5:14; 1 Corinthians 15:45, 47). He came to live among us just as we have to live. Jesus is the Creator of the human family and its Source of life. Therefore, Jesus' life is of infinite worth. His death could pay the penalty for sin and make life available to all who so choose (1 Corinthians 15:3). Jesus substituted His life for each one of us. He died in our place.

What does it mean that Jesus "took our humanity for all eternity"?
What is meant by the phrase that Jesus became the "Second Adam"?

None of us would choose to be born on a rebellious planet, but many years ago the Godhead took the penalty of our sins upon Themselves. When Jesus died on the cross, He paid the penalty for all people, for all time. The death of Jesus provided the opportunity for each of us to choose whether to obey God or Satan. If we accept Him as our Savior and Lord, God will forgive us completely, grant us eternal life, and adopt us into His family! This is the plan of salvation.

As we study the Bible, we discover that the plan of salvation is very broad. It involves three general areas:

1. Salvation from the penalty of sin.
2. Salvation from the power of sin.
3. Salvation from the effects of sin.

In this lesson we studied the Godhead's plan to deliver us from the penalty of sin through the incarnation and death of Jesus. Most of the lessons in our book deal with how Jesus delivers us from the power of sin. The last lesson will close with a study of the second coming of Jesus, when He will forever remove His people from all the effects of sin.

CHANGING TO BECOME LIKE GOD

Journal

- Explain the plan of salvation in your own words. What does it mean to you?

- What is it like to know you're completely forgiven of everything you've ever done wrong?

Dig a Little Deeper

1. The Bible has a great deal to say about sin.
   a. How many human beings are affected by sin? Romans 3:23; 1 John 1:8–10
   b. How do our self-centered natures affect us? Genesis 6:5; Mark 7:21–23
   c. What judgment hangs over our sinful race? Genesis 2:17; Romans 5:12; 6:23

2. Although God must judge and rid the universe from sin, how does He feel about lost sinners? Romans 5:8–10; 1 John 4:9, 10

3. When did the Godhead devise the plan to save sinners? 1 Corinthians 2:7; Ephesians 1:3, 4

4. In order for God the Son to accomplish His mission on earth and become the head of the human family, what mysterious change in His person was necessary? John 1:1, 14; Hebrews 2:14, 17

5. For what express purpose did Jesus come to earth? Matthew 20:28; Hebrews 2:9; Philippians 2:5–8

6. Why is God able to accept and forgive sinners who accept Jesus as Savior and Lord? Romans 3:23–26; Isaiah 53:6; 1 Corinthians 15:3; 1 Peter 3:18

7. What step must I take to restore and establish a relationship with God? Matthew 11:28–30; John 1:12

8. Long before Jesus came to live on earth, the prophet Isaiah wrote about Him.
   a. How did the prophet say Jesus would be treated and why? Isaiah 53:3–6
   b. How did this come true? Galatians 4:4, 5

9. Satan argues that if he is to be destroyed because of his sins, so should we, for we have sinned too. How does the Bible answer this? Romans 8:1, 31–33

10. God inspired Ellen White to explain that the life and death of Christ had an even broader and deeper purpose than to save His human family. Read the passage below; then write in your own words what that broader purpose was.

> "The plan of redemption had a yet broader and deeper purpose than the salvation of man. It was not for this alone that Christ came to the earth; it was not merely that the inhabitants of this little world might regard the law of God as it should be regarded; but it was to vindicate [defend successfully against any charge] the character of God before the universe. . . . The act of Christ in dying for the salvation of man would not only make heaven accessible to men, but before all the universe it would justify God and His Son in their dealing with the rebellion of Satan" (*Patriarchs and Prophets*, pp. 68, 69).

Activities

A. Make a poster with two headings: "God's Natural Laws" and "God's Moral Laws." Illustrate both kinds of laws using line drawings, symbols, or pictures.
B. Create a poem about the plan of salvation. Select a style of poetry; then plan and write your poem.
C. Listen to a recording of "Behold the Lamb of God," chorus No. 22, Handel's *Messiah*. Write your reaction to the music. Is there other music that carries this same message about Jesus?
D. Compile a list of instances in which God superseded known physical laws, e.g., multiplying loaves and fishes, coin found in mouth of fish, sun standing still. Give the Bible reference for the incident or the time in history that the event happened if it is after biblical times.

To Learn More

The Bible Story, vol. 1, pp. 61–77
The Desire of Ages, chap. 78
Messiah, chap. 78

CHANGING TO BECOME LIKE GOD

Memory Verse

"People who conceal their sins will not prosper, but if they confess and turn from them, they will receive mercy" (Proverbs 28:13).

A doctor who was examining a small boy noticed a number of scars on his hands and face. The boy's mother explained that although he often hurt himself and had even broken some bones, he never cried or complained. Tests revealed the boy had no sense of pain. One of his most important defenses against injury was missing.

Pain is a warning sign God has built into our bodies, and is an important protection for our physical health and survival. Guilt is also a warning signal. It tells us something is morally or spiritually wrong.

You have chosen Christ as your Savior and want to follow Him, but you make so many mistakes, sometimes the same mistakes. You feel so guilty! How can Christ still love you?

Jesus gives us an answer to that question in this lesson.

The Problem of Guilt

Matthew 26:69–75
Luke 22:54–62

J ennifer looked at the floor and then spoke firmly, "I didn't do it. It was already here when I came in."

"If that's the case, do you have any idea how this happened?" Mrs. Jamison asked.

"No. I just came in here and saw the writing," replied Jennifer.

"Right now we both need to get back to class. But something has to be done about the writing. If it stays here, more damage might occur. I would like to talk with you about this during lunch recess. Will you come to my office when you finish your lunch?" Mrs. Jamison asked as she turned to leave.

Back in the classroom, Jennifer tried to concentrate on her math assignment. Her thoughts kept turning to the writing in the restroom. Questions raced through her mind. *What if Mrs. Jamison doesn't believe me? What if the teacher calls my parents? Is it too late to tell the truth? Why did I do this, anyway? I already said I don't know anything about the writing. Now there are both the writing and the lie. . . .*

Mr. Donaldson interrupted her thoughts. "It seems that you are having a little trouble getting started on your assignment. Is there something you don't understand?"

"No, it's OK. I just need to get busy," she replied. Jennifer tried to concentrate on math, but the guilt she was feeling crowded her mind. Lunch came too quickly, and she knew she would soon meet with Mrs. Jamison. Tacos, usually her favorite lunch, didn't taste the same that day.

"Thank you for coming in," Mrs. Jamison greeted her. "Please sit down."

Quietly taking a chair, Jennifer tried to look confident.

"Before we get started, let's pray about this situation, OK?"

She nodded.

CHANGING TO BECOME LIKE GOD

"Gracious Father, You have promised to give us wisdom when we ask. That's what I am asking for right now. I pray for wisdom for Jennifer and for me as we talk together. Thank You for Your promises, Your love, and Your leading. In Jesus' name, Amen.

"Jennifer I've checked with the other teachers. There were a couple of students who were out of class, but not for very long. Are you sure about what you told me earlier?"

"I told you the writing was already there when I came in," Jennifer began. "But that's not the truth. I don't know why I even did it. It just sort of happened. Then you walked in, and I didn't know what to do. I know I'm in a lot of trouble. I wrote on the wall, and then I lied to you. All during math and lunch I felt so guilty. Are you going to call my parents?"

"Jennifer, I know it took courage to admit what you did. Thank you for being honest with me. Let's deal with first things first. We need to get the writing off the wall. I will call Mrs. Dean to see if there is something that will remove the writing. You can help her. Would you like for me to call your parents, or would you like to talk with them yourself? If you prefer, you can write a note to your parents and discuss it with them this evening. You can let me know after we get this cleaned up." Mrs. Jamison rose from her chair and opened the door for Jennifer.

"Mrs. Jamison, I know I'm in a lot of trouble. And I am sorry. This may seem strange, but I don't think I feel as bad as I did at lunch. You don't have to worry about me doing anything like this again," Jennifer responded.

Guilt is real. There is a difference between feeling guilty and being guilty. When people do something wrong, they are guilty. Everyone is guilty at some time. Feeling guilty warns us that something is wrong, and that warning is a good thing. When the Holy Spirit prompts us and nudges our consciences, we feel the pain of guilt and realize that we have disobeyed God. We can't run away, can't pretend it doesn't exist; we have to do something about it.

Often we try to cover up what we have done, blame someone else, or make up for it in some way. Guilty feelings make us ashamed of ourselves, and we don't like ourselves very well. We know there will be consequences, and we're afraid of what they might be.

Has the thought of the consequences kept you from an action?

There is another feeling of guilt called false guilt. It is based on a failure to believe that God forgives us. We may experience false guilt when Satan whispers discouraging things to us, such as, "Think of all the terrible things you've done. God will never forgive you," or "You're a failure. You might as well stop trying to be a Christian."

"The enemy will tempt you to think that you have done things that have separated you from God and that He no longer loves you, but our Lord loves [you] still. . . . He cares for you. He . . . will give you His peace" (Ellen G. White, *That I May Know Him*, p. 285).

Some people are never really sure that God has forgiven them for wrongs they have done. They are not convinced God's Word can be believed. Remember, it is Satan who makes us think that God doesn't love His guilty children. Remember John 3:16 and 17? "God loved the world so much that he gave his one and only Son, so that everyone who believes in him will not perish but have eternal life. God sent his Son into the world not to judge the world, but to save the world through him." The Bible says the cost of sin was the sacrifice of God's Son on Calvary. "In fact, according to the law of Moses, nearly everything was purified with blood. For without the shedding of blood, there is no forgiveness" (Hebrews 9:22).

God's love for us is not based on our behavior. He loves us because we are His children and He is our Father. When we are truly sorry for having done something wrong, we can confess the wrong we have done—and the broken relationship will be restored. Praying for forgiveness of all my sins is not an honest confession but asking forgiveness for specific sins is.

There is no way to change the past. Angry words cannot be taken back. Gossip cannot be erased. But damaged things can sometimes be repaired even though they can never be new again. Stolen property can be returned or replaced. Cruel actions can be replaced by kind ones. Lies can be replaced with truth.

Have you ever been affected by someone's lies? How did it feel?

If we are genuinely sorry for having hurt someone, we will confess not only to God but also to the one we have hurt. We will not wait for someone else to make the first move. We will do our best to make things right—not from fear of punishment but because we have hurt someone and misrepresented God.

Remember Peter's experience that night Jesus was on trial for His life? Peter had boasted that even though others would fail, he would never desert Christ. Jesus had said, " 'Peter, let me tell you something. Before the rooster crows tomorrow morning, you will deny three times that you even know me' "

(Luke 22:34). Later, when a girl recognized Peter as one of Jesus' disciples, Peter's response was, "Woman, I don't even know him!"

A second person said, "You must be one of them!"

"No, man, I'm not!" Peter retorted.

In about an hour another insisted Peter must be one of the disciples because he was a Galilean.

"Peter said, 'Man, I don't know what you are talking about.'" The words were just out of his mouth when he heard the rooster crow.

"Then Peter remembered that the Lord had said, 'Before the rooster crows tomorrow morning, you will deny three times that you even know me'" (Luke 22:57–61).

Peter, who had vowed his love and loyalty to Jesus, realized his weakness. "With the curses still on his lips and the sound of the rooster still in his ears, Peter's eyes were drawn to where Jesus stood in the hall. At that moment, Jesus turned and looked at Peter—not with anger, but with pity and deep sadness" (*Messiah,* p. 377).

"Peter left the courtyard, weeping bitterly" (Luke 22:62).

Instead of anger and reproof on Jesus' face, Peter saw pity, sorrow, love, and forgiveness. Jesus' love broke Peter's heart. Peter, the big, strong fisherman, rushed from the courtyard. He ran to the Gethsemane garden, where he threw himself on the ground and prayed for forgiveness.

Forgiven. Jesus understands human beings, sinners who want to do right but do those things that are wrong.

CHANGING TO BECOME LIKE GOD

Journal

• Reflect on a time when you failed to follow through on a promise you made. What was the reaction of the person to whom you made the promise? How did you feel?

Dig a Little Deeper

1. What assurances are found in the following texts? Briefly state what those key phrases mean for you.
   a. Psalm 103:12
   b. Isaiah 26:3
   c. John 3:17

2. Confession of guilt includes more than saying, "I'm sorry." What additional actions show the confession is genuine? Refer to 1 Peter 3:9–12 and Matthew 5:23, 24.

3. Read Luke 5:17–24, the story of the man who was let down through the roof for Jesus to heal him.
   a. What did Jesus say to the man?
   b. What did the Jewish leaders think when they heard these words?
   c. Why did Jesus use these words?

4. What does the following passage say about trying to evade guilt by using excuses such as, "Everyone does it," "No one will ever find out," or "It's a weakness I've inherited"?

   "The impenitent [those who are not sorry for sin] sometimes excuse themselves by saying of professed Christians, 'I am as good as they are.' . . . They make the faults of others an excuse for their own neglect of duty. But the sins and defects of others do not excuse anyone" (*Steps to Christ*, p. 32).

5. The Bible contains the record of a number of individuals who confessed something they had done that was wrong, but they confessed for the wrong reasons. Ellen White writes about this in *Testimonies for the Church*, volume 5, in the first paragraph that begins on page 637. Locate this passage to discover who these Bible characters were and why each one confessed his sin. Then give at least two other examples of people who confessed for the wrong reasons.

Activities

A. Suppose one of your friends says, "I feel terrible. Sometimes I think God could never love me because of the bad things I've done. I feel so guilty and I just don't know what to do." What assurance could you give your friend? Write a reply that will be an encouragement. Use John 3:16–18 and Micah 7:18, 19 to help you compose your reply.

B. Prepare a demonstration to illustrate Isaiah 1:18.

C   Write a modern-day parable about guilt and forgiveness and present it as a reader's theater.

D. Research in the *Seventh-day Adventist Hymnal* and create a poster or bulletin board based on the words of a hymn that speaks of getting rid of guilt. OR Read Romans 10:9 and rewrite it in your own words beginning, "If I confess . . ." Design a wall hanging with your personalized text, illustrate, and display.

To Learn More

The Bible Story, vol. 8, pp. 116–120; vol. 9, pp. 82–87
The Bible Pageant (1986), vol. 4, pp.151, 152
The Desire of Ages, chap. 75
The Bible Pageant, chap. 75

CHANGING TO BECOME LIKE GOD

Memory Verse

"Consecrate yourself to God in the morning; make this your very first work. Let your prayer be, 'Take me, O Lord, as wholly Thine. I lay all my plans at Thy feet. Use me today in Thy service. Abide with me, and let all my work be wrought in Thee.' This is a daily matter. Each morning consecrate yourself to God for that day. Surrender all your plans to Him, to be carried out or given up as His providence shall indicate. Thus day by day you may be giving your life into the hands of God, and thus your life will be molded more and more after the life of Christ" (Steps to Christ, p. 70).

Paul tells us that those who become Christians become new persons. They are not the same anymore, for "the old life is gone; a new life has begun!" (2 Corinthians 5:17). How does Jesus make us new? What does He do? How does He do it? Why does He do it? How do you become a Christian? How do you maintain your Christian experience?

A New Heart

Ezekiel 36:26, 27
2 Corinthians 3:18

Eighteen-year-old Dustin lay in his hospital bed thinking over the events of the past few months. Until recently, he had been a star player on his academy basketball team. He was also planning on competing in the track meet and hoping to break the record in the 400-meter race. Now he was lying in a hospital bed. How could this be happening to him?

His thoughts returned to the day he had been playing basketball and suddenly fell to the gym floor. The next thing he remembered was the hospital emergency room and the doctor telling him and his parents that he had a heart problem. Dustin had noticed that he often had trouble breathing when playing hard, but he thought he was just tired.

Numerous medical tests revealed a heart transplant was necessary, so Dustin and his parents went through the evaluation process. After much consideration, Dustin chose to sign the consent forms.

A social worker explained post-transplant life. Dustin would remain in the hospital until tests showed that his body was not rejecting the new heart. He would be required to take medications—including the anti-rejection medicine, which he would have to take the rest of his life. Now he was ready to go home to wait for a new heart. The next few days gave Dustin more time to think. He thought about his other heart transplant. When Dustin was fourteen, Jesus had given him a new heart to replace his sinful one.

Have you ever wished for a new heart?

Have you ever wondered how to become a Christian?

Have you ever wondered, "What must I do to be saved"?

Daily you learn about Jesus through personal devotions, Bible study, and prayer. The Holy Spirit influences your mind, filling your heart with love for God. Then you begin to realize how much your heavenly Father loves you.

CHANGING TO BECOME LIKE GOD

Understanding what God did for you through the death of Jesus, you will be convinced that you are a sinner. Realizing this, you will be led to repentance, a sorrow for sins, and a willingness to stop sinning. If you allow Jesus into your life, He will take away your sinful motives, desires, and thoughts, replacing them with His set of goals for your life. You will begin to love God more and want to have your own way less.

Because you have confessed your sins and determined to allow God to have control in your life, He will do the following things for you:

1. Forgive you of all your sins because Jesus' death has paid the penalty for them (1 John 1:9).
2. Trade Jesus' righteousness for your sin (2 Corinthians 5:21; Romans 4:5, 6).
3. Give you the gift of eternal life (1 John 5:11–13).
4. Adopt you into His family as a beloved son or daughter (1 John 3:1, 2; Ephesians 1:5).

Ellen White summarizes this good news of God's gift to us in the following paragraph:

"It was possible for Adam, before the fall, to form a righteous character by obedience to God's law. But he failed to do this, and because of his sin our natures are fallen and we cannot make ourselves righteous. Since we are sinful, unholy, we cannot perfectly obey the holy law. We have no righteousness of our own with which to meet the claims of the law of God. But Christ has made a way of escape for us. He lived on earth amid trials and temptations such as we have to meet. He lived a sinless life. He died for us, and now He offers to take our sins and give us His righteousness. If you give yourself to Him, and accept Him as your Saviour, then, sinful as your life may have been, for His sake you are counted righteous. Christ's character stands in place of your character, and you are accepted before God just as if you had not sinned" (*Steps to Christ,* p. 62).

?

Isn't this an amazing gift?

When God forgives you, He justifies you. Justification simply means that God has acquitted or pardoned you from all charges of sin. He has pronounced you righteous in Jesus. Justification by faith means that you believe that God has done for you what He has promised. Your salvation from sin is God's gift to you. The perfect life that Jesus lived and His death on the cross substitute for your sinful life. You receive the gift by faith when you accept Jesus as your Savior and Lord.

In what way is the life and death of Jesus a substitute for you?

One night Jesus told Nicodemus, "'I tell you the truth, unless you are born again, you cannot see the Kingdom of God'" (John 3:3). "To be born again" describes the miraculous change that takes place when you accept Jesus as your Savior and Lord. Sometimes the Bible describes this experience as receiving a new heart. When the Spirit puts love, faith, and repentance toward God in your heart, your inward thinking and motives are changed. You will want to grow and develop your Christian experience. Sharing your happiness with others will help you grow into a sturdy Christian.

What does "to be born again" mean?

The moment you accept Jesus as your Savior and Lord, God separates you from the world and claims you as His own. From that moment you begin to be more like Jesus. The process of sanctification has begun.

These expressions—new birth, justification, sanctification—describe the process of accepting Jesus as your Savior and Lord and living the Christian life. As you grow in spiritual maturity, you will make mistakes. But remember that your growing always takes place under the umbrella of God's grace. As long as you remain committed to Christ, His atoning death continues to provide forgiveness for you.

As sinners we face the final day of judgment. The penalty is certain. The wages of sin is death—eternal death. But the Bible proclaims good news— the Judge Himself has paid the penalty of death. He offers you pardon full and free—a new heart and a rewarding life with Him! Why not come to Jesus—now?

CHANGING TO BECOME LIKE GOD

Journal

- What goals and values do you have for your new life in Christ? How has God helped you to change your life into the likeness of Christ?

Dig a Little Deeper

1. Sin has been a problem for the human family since Adam and Eve first disobeyed God. Who has sinned? What are the wages (results) of sin? What is the gift of God to sinners? Romans 3:23; 6:23

2. During the time the Israelites were traveling from Egypt to Canaan, snakes were sent among them and many people died. God provided a way for those who were bitten to be healed. Numbers 21:4–9
   a. On what basis were the dying people healed (verse 9)?
   b. How did Jesus apply this experience to Himself and the salvation of sinners? John 3:14–17

3. Jesus told a parable of the Pharisee and the tax collector in Luke 18:10–14.
   a. List the good deeds the Pharisee was doing and the bad things he abstained from. Would you like to have him and his family as friends or neighbors?
   b. Is it wrong to do good deeds and to abstain from bad ones? If not, why didn't Jesus praise the Pharisee? Read Galatians 2:16. What was the Pharisee hoping to earn? Were his motives right? Why couldn't he achieve his goal?
   c. Why was the tax collector justified since he had no good works to offer God?

4. Second Corinthians 3:18 holds the key to a changed life. Compare this verse in your Bible with the version given below:

   "We all, with unveiled face, beholding the glory of the Lord, are being changed into his likeness from one degree of glory to another; for this comes from the Lord who is the Spirit" (RSV).

   a. Who is included in the words "we all" (RSV)?
   b. What phrase tells us how the change process begins?
   c. From whom does the change come?
   d. What change takes place?

Activities

A. Revelation 3:20 uses a figure of speech to describe a personal scene: Jesus stands knocking at the door of someone's heart. Read the verse from several versions and try to visualize the setting—the door, the look on Jesus' face, the person inside the door listening to the knocking and deciding what to do. Imagine what might be said between Jesus and the person inside. Write a brief imaginary conversation, expressing the feelings both of Jesus and of the person inside.

B. Interview two or three church members who have had interesting/encouraging conversion experiences. Record these interviews to share with the class.

C. Locate a print of Sallman's picture "Christ at Heart's Door" on the Internet. Consider the following questions as you analyze the picture and the metaphor it represents.
    1. Look through the grill on the door; what do you see on the inside?
    2. What image is created by the highlighting of the frame of the door and the luminescence of Christ?
    3. What is the significance of no doorknob on the outside of the door?
    4. What does this picture mean to you?

D. Using texts from this lesson, prepare a Bible study to share with someone who wants to know what to do to be saved.

To Learn More

Patriarchs and Prophets, pp. 428–432
Steps to Christ, pp. 23, 49–75

10

CHANGING TO BECOME LIKE GOD

"Faith is the confidence that what we hope for will actually happen; it gives us assurance about things we cannot see" (Hebrews 11:1).

Faith is a word that is used over and over in the Bible. What does the word *faith* mean? It is not just a warm feeling down deep in your heart. It is not blindly believing some religious idea just because somebody says you should. It is not a "leap in the dark" in the desperate hope that something might be true. Faith is not trying to make yourself believe something that you have good cause to doubt. If it isn't any or all of these things, what is faith?

Faith: Taking God at His Word

Matthew 14:22–34

A small boat tosses wildly in the darkness of a storm on the Sea of Galilee. All night long the disciples have been struggling at the oars, face to face with death. They are tired, discouraged, and afraid. Imagine James shouting to John above the howling wind, "If only the Master were here! He would help us."

Suddenly the disciples saw Someone walking toward them across the white-capped waves. They cried out in terror at such a mysterious sight. But then, across the billows they heard a familiar voice calling, "Don't be afraid. . . . Take courage. I am here!" It was the voice of Jesus.

Peter answered first. "Lord, if it's really You, tell me to come to You, walking on the water." Joy and hope and faith were all mingled in his request.

How did Peter demonstrate faith?

Suppose Jesus had said, "Peter, I'm astonished. Such a foolish thing to ask tonight! Someday when the sea is calm, perhaps you might try walking on the water, but in this terrible storm? Impossible!" Does that sound like Jesus? No! He said, "Yes, come!" Just that word *come* was enough for Peter. He dropped his oar and began to climb over the side of the boat.

Can't you imagine Andrew reaching out to stop his impetuous brother? And Thomas saying, "Who ever heard of a man walking on water! It can't be done. You'll drown!"

But Peter didn't stop. He knew that he could trust Jesus, so he climbed over the edge of the boat, stepped out upon the stormy sea, and walked.

He did not walk far, but that was his fault, not his Lord's. Perhaps Peter felt proud of his accomplishment and looked back to see whether the others were properly impressed. But when he stopped looking at Jesus, Peter suddenly became aware of the wind and waves around him. He was terrified.

At that very moment he began to sink, but even in his fright, Peter was

CHANGING TO BECOME LIKE GOD

straightforward and honest. He did not say, "It's nobody's business," or, "I'll fight it out by myself." He prayed.

Why did Peter start to sink?

His earnest prayer was short and to the point. "Save me, Lord!" Peter made no excuse. He knew that he was going to drown unless he received help. His prayer was a confession of desperate need and faith in his Master.

And what happened?

"Jesus immediately reached out and grabbed him." And Peter the proud, who had walked and sunk, rose as Peter the humble; and hand in hand with Jesus, walked again on the stormy sea.

This same Master who saved Peter on Galilee is just as ready to help you and me if we will pray in faith as Peter did!

What does it mean to pray in faith? What is faith?

That's one of the greatest questions people have been asking ever since the world was young. Thousands of books have been written about faith. Thousands of sermons have been preached to explain it. Thousands of Bible students have studied its meaning. No one can fully understand or explain all there is to know about faith, but we can know the most important things about it.

Faith is having enough confidence in God, based on the evidence He has given us, to believe what He says, to accept what He offers, and to do what He tells us to do, no matter what happens. It is being absolutely convinced that God will keep His promise to give us new hearts and new minds. When we deliberately and thoughtfully choose to believe God, we are really saying, "I know You're my Friend. I want to be Your friend too. From now on You are my God. I will serve and love You."

What are some words you can use to describe faith?

God has more to offer us than we can imagine. He offers to take care of us. He offers to be with us every day and to help us grow more like Him. He tells us that He loves us and that He wants us to be with Him forever in the new earth He is going to create. But God doesn't ask us to trust Him without knowing Him, so He has given us evidence in His Word that what He tells us is the truth.

Peter demonstrated his faith that long-ago day on the stormy sea. So did many other people whose experiences are recorded in the Bible.

Hebrews 11 contains a record of many people who demonstrated much faith in God. Most of the names you probably know: Abel, Noah, Abraham. Others you may not know, such as Barak and Jephthah. Some names, such as Samson, you may be surprised to find there. A number of other people are described but are not even named. Paul tells us that all of the men and women who are mentioned were included for one special reason. They all had faith in God.

The question is, "How can we have faith like theirs?" First of all, we must get acquainted with God. By watching Him in action through the stories of the Bible, we will soon discover that He is our Friend. A person who doesn't trust God, either doesn't know Him personally or doesn't choose to be His friend. When we are close to Him, we discover we can trust Him.

"Faith comes from hearing, that is, hearing the Good News about Christ" (Romans 10:17), Paul said. In his day, it was the custom for people to go to synagogues or to meet in homes or even out-of-doors and listen to someone read the Scriptures out loud for everyone to hear. If Paul were living today, when almost everyone can own a Bible, he might say, "Faith comes by reading the Bible."

Why is faith more dependable than feeling?

Faith has its foundation in the Bible. Faith claims God's promises and results in obedience. It is not enough to believe about Christ; we must believe in Him and accept Him as a personal Savior. Faith is not a feeling. It is not foolish or overconfident and does not take God for granted. Faith is a two-way agreement by which those who accept Christ join themselves in partnership with Him. Faith means trust.

By allowing God to give us His righteousness, He is able to set us right and keep us right with Him. Our willingness to let Him do this, and our confidence that He is able to do so, is evidence that we trust Him. Our faith in God and His grace as is manifested in our daily works and in our walk with Him makes it possible for Him to rescue us from this troubled planet. As a result, we can live in safety and perfect happiness with Him, forever.

A young boy traveling on an airplane was asked by a flight attendant if he was ever afraid while flying. He replied, "Not with this pilot! I trust him. He is my father!"

How about you? Do you know your heavenly Father well enough to know that you can trust Him?

CHANGING TO BECOME LIKE GOD

Journal

- Write a few sentences giving your definition and understanding of *faith.* Tell how you demonstrate faith. Why do you have confidence in God?

Dig a Little Deeper

1. How can your faith in God be developed even though you've never seen Him? Romans 10:17; John 14:6–9

2. Hebrews 11 can be called God's Hall of Faith. What acts of faith are given for each of the following: Abel, Noah, Abraham, Jacob, Moses, Rahab?

3. Suppose a person you didn't know very well asked you to agree to do whatever he requested.
   a. Would you comply? Why or why not?
   b. If you were afraid of him, how would you feel about doing what he asked?
   c. How can you learn whether you can trust someone?
   d. How can you demonstrate to someone else that he or she can trust you?
   e. How can you know that you can trust God?

4. Review the story of Gideon and his request for a sign from God. Why did Gideon ask for a second sign from God? How did God help Gideon develop faith? Judges 6:1–6, 11, 12, 36–40

5. Write at least four ideas that add to your understanding of the meaning of faith.
   a. Matthew 9:27–31
   b. Acts 16:30, 31
   c. Galatians 3:26; Hebrews 11:1
   d. "Faith is trusting God—believing that He loves us and knows best what is for our good" (*Education*, p. 253).
   e. "Our faith must be an intelligent faith, looking unto Jesus in perfect confidence" (*Selected Messages*, bk. 1, p. 256).
   f. Faith makes a change in the believer. Belief that does not make changes in a person's life is not real faith (adapted from Ellen G. White Comments, *SDA Bible Commentary,* vol. 7, p. 936).

Activities

A. Prepare a "hall of faith" display honoring the men and women of Hebrews 11. Include a picture and brief paragraph describing why each individual qualifies.

B. Which example below reveals greater faith in God? Have a panel discussion in which some students defend each of the following:
   1. "I know I'll be healed, for I have faith God will answer my prayer."
   2. "I don't know what God will do, but I know that I can trust Him. Whether He heals me or not has nothing to do with my faith in Him."

C. Create a Haiku that expresses faith and praise. Illustrate.

D. Some people say they do not, or cannot, have faith. Yet these people show faith every day of their lives. For example, they do not worry if they will never see the sun again when it goes down at night. They have faith that it will rise again the next morning. Why do they have faith the sun will rise in the morning?

   Make a list of several ways in which you show faith each day. Why do you have faith that each of these items will happen? How can you experience a faith relationship with God? Compare your list with those of your classmates.

To Learn More

The Bible Pageant (1986), vol. 2, pp. 159–165; vol. 4, pp. 97, 98
The Bible Story, vol. 3, pp. 115–123; vol. 10, pp. 157–160

11

CHANGING TO BECOME LIKE GOD

Memory Verse

"Prayer is the opening of the heart to God as to a friend. Not that it is necessary in order to make known to God what we are, but in order to enable us to receive Him. Prayer does not bring God down to us, but brings us up to Him" (Steps to Christ, *p. 93*).

"When Jesus was upon the earth, He taught His disciples how to pray. He directed them to present their daily needs before God, and to cast all their care upon Him. And the assurance He gave them that their petitions should be heard, is assurance also to us" (*Steps to Christ*, p. 93).

Keeping in Touch With God

1 John 1:9; Matthew 6:5–13

Mike Copithorne was a world-class wakeboarder and snowboarder. As a professional athlete and full-time student at Pacific Union College, he was living his greatest dream. Even though the people he associated with placed their emphasis on the "here and now," God had been speaking to Mike, reminding him of the truths he had learned at home and at school. He had led Mike to make a commitment and to renew the friendship he had discovered in Jesus.

Easter weekend 2000 found Mike snowboarding with his friends on the slopes of Mammoth Mountain. Taking off from the jump, he realized immediately that he was not going to land this one. Mike's instincts were correct. He landed wrong, and, as a result, he was paralyzed from the waist down. He spent the next few weeks in the hospital in an intensive rehabilitation program. Three days after Mike was released from the hospital, his dad passed away suddenly from a heart attack. This was more than he could handle alone.

Mike came face to face with the reality that his life had changed forever because of the accident. He also had to face the fact that his dad had died. Mike turned to God to get him through. He says, "What the world sees as a curse, God sees as an opportunity." Today Mike is a teacher in an Adventist school. He still enjoys fly-fishing, downhill mountain biking, white-water rafting, various snow activities, and traveling around the world with his wife, Carrie. He reminds us that God has a plan. "He is the Friend that was there with me at the height of my success and through the lowest and darkest times of my life. I know that He will do the same for you. He had a plan for my life and He has a plan for you. Take time to get to know Him and listen to His voice."

But how do we listen to God's voice? How do we talk with Him and hear

CHANGING TO BECOME LIKE GOD

His answers? What is prayer? How can it become a personal conversation between us and God? Prayer is one way we respond to God, who communicates with us through His Word, through the Holy Spirit, through nature, and through the events in our lives. It is the opening of the heart to God in the same way we talk with a close friend.

? *Would it still be praying if you wrote your prayer in a journal?*

You may be thinking that not all prayers you have heard sounded like someone talking with a friend. Some of those prayers may have sounded very formal, not at all the way you would address a friend. Some prayers are more formal because the setting or the occasion is more formal.

Dr. Barry Black, a rear admiral, the 62nd chaplain of the United States Senate, is the first military chaplain, the first African American, and the first Seventh-day Adventist to serve in this capacity. Read the following prayer he offered after the Senate was called to order on Thursday, October 6, 2005.

"Gracious God, sustainer of our lives, rescue us from the faults to which we are so prone. Keep us from saying one thing and doing another. Save us from criticizing in others what we condone in ourselves. Deliver us from demanding of others standards we make no effort to fulfill. Give us wisdom not to flirt with temptation but to avoid even the near occasion to sin. Protect us from an indecision that can't say yes or no and from a reluctance to break habits we know are wrong.

"Bless our Senators today. Keep them from trying to please both others and You. Save us all from anything which would keep us from loving You with all our heart, soul, mind, and strength.

"We pray in Your Holy Name. Amen."*

? *How does this prayer for legislators differ from what was prayed in your classroom today?*

While this prayer is indeed a petition, it may be much more formal in language and structure than what you pray with your family or in your classroom. Why is this so? Think about the formality and ceremony that accompany Senate proceedings. The prayer is appropriate for the setting and the audience. But is the request, the intent so different? Does the prayer invite God to speak to us? Does it invite Him to lead our lives so that they are in agreement with His will?

What is the primary purpose of prayer? Is it to seek God's will? Is it to ask God for things we want or need? Is it to change God's mind? Could it be to change us? Jesus talked about the importance of prayer. He said in Matthew 18:20, "Where two or three gather together as my followers, I am there among them."

God is with us in prayer. What a marvelous promise! We have the listening ear of the God of the universe. But even though God is available, even though He is present, at times we may encounter such a difficult situation that we don't even know how to pray. We don't know what to ask. We don't know what could make the situation bearable. How can we pray when we don't even have the words?

"The Holy Spirit helps us in our weakness. For example, we don't know what God wants us to pray for. But the Holy Spirit prays for us with groanings that cannot be expressed in words" (Romans 8:26). God has promised to be with us. He has promised to send His Holy Spirit to speak for us in our prayers. God never tires of hearing our worries, our joys, and our questions. He knows how these can bother or annoy or worry us. We need never hesitate or feel ashamed to come to Him. He knows exactly what we need. He understands that we have done wrong. He provided the Sacrifice for our sin. When we confess, He forgives us. He gives the strength needed to endure or to change.

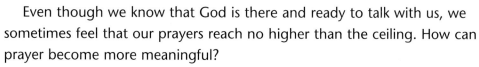

If God already knows our mistakes and sins, why should we confess them?

Even though we know that God is there and ready to talk with us, we sometimes feel that our prayers reach no higher than the ceiling. How can prayer become more meaningful?

Here are some suggestions that may help:

1. Choose a time for prayer when you are not tired or hurried.
2. Ask the Holy Spirit to help you keep your mind from wandering.
3. Be specific in your prayers. Thank God for specific blessings He has given you, ask for particular sins to be forgiven, tell God the exact concern you have about yourself and others.
4. Even if you are alone, it may help to pray out loud. It may be easier to focus on praying when you say the words instead of just thinking them.
5. If you usually write down what is important to you, try writing your prayers.

6. If you feel you are constantly repeating the same requests over and over, read a passage in the Bible and talk with God about what you have read.

7. Take time to think about God and listen for that still, small Voice. We do not come to know God by rushing off too quickly.

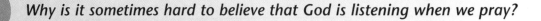

Why is it sometimes hard to believe that God is listening when we pray?

Paul presents another aspect of prayer in 1 Thessalonians 5:17, where he says to "never stop praying." The King James Version says to "pray without ceasing." How can one pray continually or never stop praying? The closer one comes to God, the more that person looks to God in every situation. As things arise throughout the day, the thoughts automatically turn to God, asking for His guidance, His leading. "We may keep so near to God that in every unexpected trial our thoughts will turn to Him as naturally as the flower turns to the sun" (*Steps to Christ,* pp. 99, 100). In each aspect of our daily living, we bring the weighty matters as well as the small ones to Him. We continually direct our thoughts to God.

Does God answer prayers? This is the question you may have asked your-self, especially if you have prayed for something important, really important, and nothing seemed to happen. Sometimes we do not recognize that our prayers have been answered because the answer was not what we wanted or expected. Consider the way parents answer requests made by their children.

You are loved by the most powerful, most awesome Being in the universe. That concept may be difficult to wrap your mind around. God loves you more than you can imagine. He always wants what is best for you.

"But," you may be asking, "if God wants what is best for me, if He loves me so dearly, why did He allow my parents to get divorced?" Or perhaps you have wondered why a loving God did not heal a loved one or protect some-one from an accident. Why did He let our house catch fire? Why did He let my dog get run over? Why did He let me fail that test? Why? Why? Why? These are the kinds of questions people have asked since the day Cain killed Abel.

In answering our prayers, God never forces people. He never forces some-one to stop drinking or to stop driving when they are drunk. God could force people. He could always perform miracles so that no one who loves Him ever gets sick or hurt or dies. God could do that. But if He did, Satan would claim that people only love God because of what God can do for them. Satan made that accusation against Job (Job 1:6–11).

Whether God answers us by saying Yes, No, Wait, or by giving us something different, He is still there loving us, wanting to lead us. We are in the middle of the great controversy between God and Satan. Satan is still on earth trying to convince us to hate and distrust God. Until Jesus comes and ends the controversy, we must live with disappointment, pain, and death. But God cares, He hears, and He is with us. He will give the courage, the peace, and the strength to face whatever comes along. We can trust God to be there.

As you spend time with God, as you pray and talk with Him, take time to listen for His voice, His still, small voice.

* *Congressional Record,* vol. 151, no. 130, Friday, October 7, 2005.

CHANGING TO BECOME LIKE GOD

Journal

- Write about a time when you prayed. How did God answer?

Dig a Little Deeper

1. Look briefly at Daniel's prayer life.
   a. How often and where did he pray? Daniel 6:10
   b. What influence did his prayer life have on the king? Daniel 6:16
   c. How did Daniel give God credit for answering his prayers? Daniel 6:22

2. After reading the following passages, write a short paragraph telling how you can show reverence to God as you talk with Him.

   "It is our duty to bow upon our knees before God when we offer our petitions to Him. Jesus, our example, 'kneeled down, and prayed.' . . . Paul declared: 'I bow my knees unto the Father of our Lord Jesus Christ.' . . . Daniel 'kneeled upon his knees three times a day, and prayed, and gave thanks before his God'" (Ellen G. White, *God's Amazing Grace*, p. 91).

   "True reverence for God is inspired by a sense of His infinite greatness and a realization of His presence. . . . Angels, when they speak that name, veil their faces. With what reverence, then, should we, who are fallen and sinful, take it upon our lips!" (*Prophets and Kings*, pp. 48, 49).

3. There is one major obstacle to prayer.
   a. What sometimes comes between us and God when we try to pray? Isaiah 59:1, 2
   b. What can we do to correct the problem? 1 John 1:9

4. God does not always answer our prayers the way we would choose to have them answered. Paul had a physical disability that he called a "thorn in the flesh" (2 Corinthians 12:7). Some Bible scholars think this "thorn" was poor eyesight. To discover how Paul handled his problem, find answers to these questions.
   a. What request did Paul make about his disability? How many times did he repeat his request? 2 Corinthians 12:8
   b. How did God respond to Paul's request? 2 Corinthians 12:9
   c. What attitude did Paul reveal regarding God's reply? Philippians 4:11
   d. Paul knew, beyond any doubt, that someday his "thorn in the flesh" would be removed. Find out when. 1 Corinthians 15:50–53
   e. Learn what Paul was sure would happen in the meantime. Philippians 4:19

5. What did the disciples ask of Jesus regarding prayer? Luke 11:1

6. What did Jesus teach His disciples to say when they prayed? Write the prayer in your own words. Luke 11:2–4; Matthew 6:9–15

7. If God knows all about us and our needs, why do we still need to pray? Read your memory verse and the following texts and quotes; then answer in your own words. Psalm 143:10; Luke 11:13

   "It is a part of God's plan to grant us, in answer to the prayer of faith, that which He would not bestow did we not thus ask" (*The Great Controversy*, p. 525).

   We do not pray so that God will know us. We pray to help us know and receive Him (adapted from *Steps to Christ,* p. 93).

Activities

A. Prepare a bulletin board or booklet about prayer. Use quotes and texts from the narrative, Dig a Little Deeper, and those listed below.
   Prayer Is
   • "the breath of the soul" (*Gospel Workers*, p. 254).
   • "the key in the hand of faith to unlock heaven's storehouse" (*Steps to Christ*, p. 94).
   • "the strength of the Christian" (*Testimonies*, vol. 1, p. 504).
   • heaven's chosen means of success in our battle against sin (adapted from *Sons and Daughters of God*, p. 335).

B. Keep a prayer diary or log. Write your requests in one column and answers in the other.

C. Search *The Seventh-day Adventist Hymnal* for hymns about prayer. When you find one that especially speaks to your heart, look up the story about the origins of the hymn in the *Companion to the Hymnal*. (For suggestions, check the section "Meditation and Prayer" in the topical index at the back of the hymnal.)

D. Interview three people concerning prayer. Ask questions such as, Can you give an example of a payer that was answered? What do you do when you find it difficult to pray? Do you have a special time or a favorite place to pray? Would you have any suggestions for making prayer more meaningful? After you complete your interviews, select a method to share your results.

To Learn More

Daniel 6:20–23
The Bible Story, vol. 8, pp. 66–69, 141–144
The Desire of Ages, chap. 73
Messiah, chap. 73

12

CHANGING TO BECOME LIKE GOD

Memory Verse

"He does not punish us for our sins; He does not deal harshly with us, as we deserve. For His unfailing love toward those who fear Him is as great as the height of the heavens above the earth. He has removed our sins as far from us as the east is from the west" (Psalm 103:10–12).

The prophet Jeremiah dealt with some very proud, rebellious people who did not obey God. Finally God sent a message to them through Jeremiah asking, "Can a leopard take away its spots? Neither can you start doing good, for you have always done evil" (Jeremiah 13:23). If Jeremiah were talking to us today, he might say, "Do you think you can change your tendency to sin? You can't do that any more than a leopard can change its spots."

Jeremiah didn't talk about spotted leopards to discourage us. But how can those spots on our characters be changed?

God Is on Our Side

John 14:13, 14

The Bible gives us many examples of how people related to God. It tells stories of individuals who seemed to always make the best choices—Enoch and Daniel. Other stories describe the lives of those who struggled to follow God. Some turned away from Him, and yet later learned to trust Him completely. What happened in the lives of these individuals that allowed them to listen to the Holy Spirit and be led to change? In this lesson we will study some examples.

Miriam loved Moses. He was the younger brother she had watched at the river's edge. Carefully and skillfully she had protected him as he rocked in the basket. When Pharaoh's daughter noticed the basket and had it drawn from the water, Miriam mustered the courage to approach her. "Would you like a Hebrew nurse to care for him?" she asked. This young girl lived the life of a slave. Never had she talked with royalty. But now her brother's life was at stake.

Miriam's support of Moses did not stop there. As Israel completed their Red Sea crossing during the Exodus from Egypt, she led them in praise to God. Taking her tambourine, she led the women in singing these words:

> Sing to the LORD
> for he has triumphed gloriously;
> he has hurled both horse and rider into the sea (Exodus 15:21).

But Miriam did not always give support to Moses. She was displeased that her brother had married Zipporah, a Cushite woman. Moses' wife saw that the burdens of leading so many people were wearing away his strength. In talking the situation over with her father, Jethro, a solution was found. Jethro suggested a method of organizing the people so Moses did not have to deal with every situation. Miriam became jealous and envious that she and Aaron had not been consulted in this decision. She assumed that Zipporah must be the reason

CHANGING TO BECOME LIKE GOD

Moses no longer took them into his confidence. Miriam murmured and complained against Moses, but in so doing, she was guilty of disloyalty to God. The Lord dealt with this jealousy and envy immediately.

Why do you think Zipporah saw the situation differently from the way Miriam did?

The story continues with Miriam suddenly contracting the most dreaded illness—leprosy. Here is where Moses' character is revealed. He immediately pleaded for God to heal her. And God answered. Miriam had fallen prey to one of the most satanic traits that can exist in the human heart, that of envy (*Patriarchs and Prophets,* p. 385). God was able to use Moses because he was teachable. As a meek person, he was willing to be instructed. Miriam confessed her sin and also learned the importance of humbling herself and following God's will.

Another story illustrating the importance of humbly following God is that of Samson. Manoah and his wife had been instructed by God that He had an important work for their son, Samson. But Samson made choices that led to a life of disappointment and shame rather than one that gave honor and glory to God. "Physically Samson was the strongest man upon the earth; but in self-control, integrity, and firmness, he was one of the weakest of men" (*Patriarchs and Prophets*, p. 567). At the end of his life, Samson made another choice. As a blind captive, he turned to God, asking Him to avenge the Philistines. No longer lacking in self-control, he surrendered all to God. Leaning against a pillar, he stretched his arms and gave a mighty pull, bringing down the entire building. He died with the Philistines. But that is not the end of what is written about Samson. Hebrews 11, the Faith Chapter, lists Samson along with Gideon, David, and Samuel.

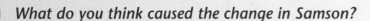

What do you think caused the change in Samson?

How were these individuals able to change their spots? How does anyone turn against the natural inclination to sin, allowing God to lead? The Holy Spirit continually speaks to us, gently suggesting how we can follow God. Paul describes our situation in Romans 3:23 when he says that all of us are sinners. He goes on to describe the cost of being a sinner as death. But then he tells us something else—that God gives us a free gift, eternal life (Romans 6:23). Accepting that free gift is called conversion. We are converted from our own sinful ways to the ways of Jesus.

Conversion creates in the person a new capacity for knowing and loving

God. It is the turning-around point, the beginning, but that's all it is. And we are told we need to be converted daily, not just once. As Jesus comes in, sin is crowded out. There is no point in trying to stamp it out ourselves. It will never work that way. It only happens by Jesus' strength being exchanged for our weaknesses that are then surmounted by His power. That's why Jesus accepts people just as they are. Only He can make the changes.

Some people seem to think that they must be good before coming to God. No wonder they become discouraged or perhaps even resentful. Some people misunderstand our loving God, who accepts them as they are. After making the decision to serve God, they receive help through the Holy Spirit to overcome sin.

Does it ever work to make the changes before coming to God?

It is encouraging to know that our characters are not determined by occasional good deeds or occasional bad ones, but by remaining in touch with Jesus. If we choose to follow Christ's instructions and example, He will give us whatever help we need.

Sometimes we must admit that we just don't want to do the right thing. The Holy Spirit is there to answer our honest prayer asking help for us to choose the right thing. The strength God gives in answer to honest prayers for help is amazing, for such prayers mean that whether we feel like it or not, we have made the decision to follow God. We are saying, as Jesus said in Matthew 26:39, "I want your will to be done, not mine." Gradually feelings change from "I ought to" to "I want to" and finally to "I will."

What is our part in developing good characters?

We can always trust God to do what He says. He loves us and promises to give us the help we need in order to succeed. He will give the strength to overcome sin. He can remove the spots. God is on our side.

CHANGING TO BECOME LIKE GOD

Journal

- Write about something you would like to overcome through Jesus.
  OR
- Write about something you overcame through Jesus.

Dig a Little Deeper

1. What important truth do we need to understand before we can begin to overcome a problem? Ephesians 2:8, 9

2. What is it that leads a person to repentance and the new way of life we call conversion? Romans 2:4

3. When God forgives us, He does so completely. We do not need to listen when Satan whispers, "What you have done is so terrible that God will never forgive you." Write the promise for sinners found in each of these tests.
   a. 1 John 4:4
   b. Zechariah 4:6
   c. John 6:37
   d. 2 Peter 3:9

4. You need to give yourself every opportunity to do right if you expect to win the war against sin. Avoid situations in which temptations can strike.
   As you cooperate with God in doing this, what has He promised to do?
   1 Corinthians 10:13; Romans 8:37; 2 Corinthians 3:18

5. The following paragraphs describe a certain kind of obedience that is acceptable to God, and another that is not. What is the difference between the two?

   > A sullen submission to the will of the Father will develop the character of a rebel. A rebel thinks of obedience as drudgery. He does not obey cheerfully nor because he loves God. Instead, his obedience is a mere mechanical performance. If he dared, he would disobey. Such a service brings no peace to the soul (adapted from Ellen G. White, *Signs of the Times,* July 22, 1897).

   > Those who attempt to keep the commandments just from a sense of obligation, because they are required to, will never find joy in obedience. True obedience is given out of loyalty and love. This will lead one to do right because it is right—because doing what is right is pleasing to God (based on *Christ's Object Lessons,* pp. 97, 98).

Activities

A. Think of a Bible character whose life provides evidence that God forgives anyone who is willing to accept forgiveness. Imagine that you are the person and make a record of your experience. This could be in the form of a short story, a diary, or a photo album of drawings with appropriate captions. If you need help in choosing a person about whom to write, these references may give you an idea.
   - Moses. Exodus 2:11; 3:1–6, 12
   - Thief on the cross. Luke 23:32, 33, 39–43
   - Paralyzed man. Mark 2:1–12
   - Woman at the well. John 4:1–15, 29, 30, 39–41
   - Man at the Pool of Bethesda. John 5:2–9; *The Desire of Ages,* pp. 202, 203

B. Select key words from this lesson or unit and construct a crossword puzzle. Use words such as *encouraging, strength*, and *prayer.*

C. Read the following scenario. Then answer the questions that follow:
   Charles was restoring his antique 1930 Model A Ford. Most of the time the project was enjoyable because car restoration was his hobby. He was usually patient and meticulous while working on the more detailed aspects. One evening, however, he was working on a stubborn engine bolt that would not loosen. He tried several different methods, such as soaking it in oil and heating it with a torch. It would not budge. Becoming impatient, he tried one last time with the wrench. Pulling with all his might, he heard a telltale crack as the bolt snapped off. As the wrench slipped off the broken bolt, his knuckles smashed into the side of the engine. Angered by the broken bolt and the pain of throbbing knuckles, he threw the wrench against the wall. The wrench slammed into the fender of his son's new bicycle, creating a large dent in the red fender. As he viewed the damage, he realized that his angry outburst had damaged his son's prized possession.
   a. What advice would you give Charles if he asked you for advice?
   b. How does Charles's behavior affect others?
   c. What advice would you give to the son?

D. Write a short skit about someone who wishes to change a habit or behavior.

To Learn More

Exodus 15
Numbers 12
Judges 13–16
Hebrews 11
The Acts of the Apostles, p. 482
Christ's Object Lessons, pp. 97, 333
Selected Messages, bk. 1, p. 336

Everyone who meets Jesus is changed. Some learn to follow His example, while others turn away. As you examine the lives of Bible characters, make the decision to become like Him.

unit 3

GETTING TO KNOW GOD

While You're Studying

A Write the memory verses for the unit and add them to your file.

B Make a "My Gift to You" coupon book with coupons that you can give to your family members, friends, church family members, or neighbors.

C Form a circle with your classmates. Each student needs to think of questions he or she would like to ask characters from this unit. Choose a soft object to pass or toss. As the object comes to you, ask your question and toss the object to another student. This activity may work best at the end of the unit.

D As a culminating activity for the unit, publish a newspaper covering the topics that were studied. Your paper could include feature articles about each of the lessons, artwork, an advice column, letters to the editor, photos, an editorial, or poetry.

© DARREL TANK

GETTING TO KNOW GOD

Memory Verse

"Commit everything you do to the LORD. Trust him, and he will help you" *(Psalm 37:5).*

Two men, much alike in many ways but very different in others, were faced with a life-changing decision. Although the circumstances were different for each man, the basic option was the same. What did Jesus ask these men to do?

Two Men: Two Decisions

Luke 5:27–32; 18:18–30

Levi Matthew was a hated and lonely man. Even though he was a Jew, few Jews would speak to him when they met him on the street. They despised him. Matthew was a tax collector for the Romans, which on the surface might seem to have been a decent enough job. The Romans, however, were an enemy force occupying Palestine, and the Jewish people abhorred paying taxes to them.

Taxmen were known for inventing dishonest schemes to make money for themselves. It was legal for them to keep everything they could get above the required tax. So tax collectors increased the amount the Jews were forced to pay. Levi Matthew was a man without friends.

In spite of his wealth, Levi Matthew was not a happy man. He had listened to Jesus and had observed how He treated people. Matthew admired this teacher from Nazareth. He wanted to be a better man and was sure that Jesus could help him. But he was afraid the great Teacher would never pay any attention to him. None of the other religious leaders did; they made it clear they wanted nothing to do with him.

Matthew sat alone in his tax booth down by the seaside. When the fishermen brought in their catch, he weighed the fish, figured the bill, and collected the taxes, always making sure he added something extra for himself.

What kind of help did Matthew want from Jesus?

Then, one day Jesus came walking by Matthew's booth and stopped. There is no record that Matthew said anything to Jesus, but Jesus had something to say to him, just two words. Two words that changed Levi Matthew's world.

"Follow me."

"So Levi got up, left everything, and followed him" (Luke 5:27, 28).

There was no hesitation, no questioning, no concern about making his living. He was through being a cheat. It was enough for Matthew that Jesus had invited him. He wanted to be with Jesus, to listen, to learn, and to unite with Jesus in His work.

Another Jewish man was eager to meet Jesus. We don't know his name, but we do know that he was young and popular. Like Matthew, he was also wealthy. He was a leader in his community and deeply devoted to his religion. He had seen Jesus and had listened to His teachings, noticing how gentle and

kind Jesus was. The more this young ruler saw of Jesus, the more he wanted to be one of His disciples. One day, when he saw Jesus coming, he ran to meet Him and knelt at His feet. "Teacher," he asked, "what good deed must I do to have eternal life?" (Matthew 19:16). Jesus told him he must obey the commandments. The young man replied, "'I've obeyed all these commandments since I was young'" (Mark 10:20).

Jesus looked at the young man with love and concern. "'There is still one thing you haven't done,'" He told him. "'Go and sell all your possessions and give the money to the poor, and you will have treasure in heaven. Then come, follow me'" (Mark 10:21).

What was the "one thing" the rich young man lacked?

That wasn't at all what the young man expected. Imagine the thoughts that must have overwhelmed him. *Why must I give up everything to follow this Teacher? Why can't I be His disciple and still keep my possessions?*

To the Jews, possessions were considered an evidence of God's blessings. Wealth was thought to be a sign of righteousness; poverty, on the other hand, was thought to be evidence that God was displeased with a person. Why would Jesus ask him to do something that would make it appear that God disapproved of him? That would be humiliating! He turned and walked sadly away. There is no record that they ever saw each other again.

The rich young ruler had thought he wanted to be Jesus' disciple, but the price was too great. His possessions and his power were his idols. "He loved the gifts God had given him more than the Giver. Being with Jesus meant less to him than being seen as rich and powerful" (*Messiah*, p. 288).

Two men. Two significant decisions. One chose wealth and position; the other gave up wealth and chose to follow Jesus.

GETTING TO KNOW GOD

Journal

- If Christ were to visit your classroom today, what might He ask you to give up in order to follow Him?

Dig a Little Deeper

1. What choice did Levi Matthew and the young ruler have to make and why? Read Matthew 6:24.

2. Jesus does not ask every wealthy person who accepts Him to give away all his or her possessions. There are many people whose wealth and influence become a great blessing. Skim *Messiah,* chapter 80, to find two wealthy people who made contributions after Jesus' death. Summarize what they did.

3. The Bible records the story of another wealthy tax collector who was also eager to follow Jesus. Write a brief summary of his encounter with Jesus. Luke 19:1–10

4. Why did the rich young ruler not follow Jesus? Read *Messiah*, chapter 57.

5. For the rich young ruler, his possessions and power were his idols. Read the following passage; then develop a definition of *idolatry.*

> "Paul urged his brethren to ask themselves what influence their words and deeds would have upon others and to do nothing, however innocent in itself, that would seem to sanction idolatry or offend the scruples of those who might be weak in the faith. 'Whether therefore ye eat, or drink, or whatsoever ye do, do all to the glory of God. Give none offense, neither to the Jews, nor to the Gentiles, nor to the church of God.'
>
> "The apostle's words of warning to the Corinthian church are applicable to all time and are especially adapted to our day. By idolatry he meant not only the worship of idols, but self-serving, love of ease, the gratification of appetite and passion. A mere profession of faith in Christ, a boastful knowledge of the truth, does not make a man a Christian. A religion that seeks only to gratify the eye, the ear, and the taste, or that sanctions self-indulgence, is not the religion of Christ" (*The Acts of the Apostles*, pp. 316, 317).

What idols do people commonly worship today?

Activities

A. Which do think is more important, giving up all your possessions or being *willing* to give up all your possessions? Why? Could you give up all your possessions and still not fulfill what Jesus was asking the rich young ruler to do? After taking a survey of your classmates, select two teams to debate this question.

B. Imagine that you are with Jesus when the young ruler comes to see Him. After Jesus tells him what he needs to do, the young man turns to you and protests. "Wait a minute! If I sell all my things, how will I have food to eat or clothes to wear?" Read Matthew 6:21, 25–34; then compose a paragraph giving a response.

C. Role-play scenes in which a news reporter is interviewing the rich young ruler and Levi Matthew. In scene one, the rich young ruler is walking down the street looking very dejected. A reporter steps up and explains that he is reporting "human interest" stories about this man Jesus, who is creating such a stir throughout the entire area of Palestine. The reporter might ask questions such as these:
   - What was it that made you interested in Jesus?
   - What did Jesus ask you to do?
   - What decision did you make? Why?
   - What do you think your family and friends will think of your decision?
   - What do you expect to be doing during the next few days/years?
   - Would you recommend that the others make the same decision you did?

   In scene two, the reporter approaches Levi Matthew, explaining that he has heard about the tax office being abandoned and wants to know what has happened. (The reporter asks Levi Matthew the same questions.)

D. Doing something special for someone else can be very rewarding, especially if you are denying yourself something by so doing. Experience this by participating in one of the following activities:
   1. Work with your teacher to begin a big brother/big sister program with lower-grade students. Here are some things you might like to do:
      - Help them with their schoolwork.
      - Play with them on the playground.
      - Assist on field trips.
      - Help new students get acquainted.
   2. Plan a "Sugar Famine." Go without candy, ice cream, dessert, or other treats for one week. Use the money saved to help a person in need.
   3. Make a sincere effort to be friendly to someone who is shy or lonely.
   4. Check your local hospitals and nursing homes to see what volunteer activities are available to students.

   Write a reflection in your journal about your experience.

To Learn More

The Bible Pageant (1986), vol. 4, pp. 108, 109
The Bible Story, vol. 9, pp. 15–18, 129–133

Memory Verse

"If we confess our sins to him, he is faithful and just to forgive us our sins and to cleanse us from all wickedness" (1 John 1:9).

The main characters in this lesson are a young woman who became an important example for every person wanting to be a Christian and a wealthy man who had a startling experience that changed him from a proud, guilty cheat to a loyal follower of Christ.

Who were these people? What happened to them? Why are their stories important to Christians today? What do the events of this lesson tell you about the kind of Person God is?

The Gospel According to Mary

Luke 7:36–56; Mark 14

There was no doubt about it: Mary was a sinner. She had a reputation all over town.

Mary hadn't always been that way. She had grown up in a good home. Her sister Martha was a capable hostess in the little town of Bethany. Her brother Lazarus was a fine citizen and a courteous host. Mary was probably a cheerful, friendly girl who made home a pleasant place.

But one sad day a man named Simon led her into immorality. Simon was able to cover up his part. He acted as if nothing had happened and went right on working as a leader in the community. But Mary could not pretend. Her self-respect was shattered. She felt guilty, a worthless nobody. In despair, Mary thought there was no choice but to continue in immorality. Once Mary made this choice, Satan took charge and, to a great extent, controlled her mind.

Why did Mary think she was a worthless sinner who was beyond hope?

Perhaps Mary moved to Magdala to save her family's reputation. Perhaps that was where she first heard the Carpenter of Nazareth talking about sin, forgiveness, healing, and a new way of life. The more Mary heard, the more she wanted to be rid of her terrible feelings of guilt. But surely a man as holy and good as Jesus would have nothing to do with her.

Believing that she was unworthy almost crushed the tiny bit of hope Jesus' words had given her. In desperation, Mary went to Jesus and cried for help. Jesus forgave her. He talked and prayed with her. And when Mary went her way, she knew that she was forgiven. It was as if Jesus said to Mary, "What you have done is wrong, but your life isn't over. I do not condemn you. Go home and do not sin again."

GETTING TO KNOW GOD

Because actions repeated over and over become habits and are not easy to change, it was not long before Mary slipped back into her sinful ways. Again and again she failed, but each time the Holy Spirit led her to Jesus for help. Each time He forgave her, and His patient kindness led her to repentance. At last, Mary became a new person.

Then Mary and Simon met again. Jesus had healed Simon of leprosy—an ugly, frightening disease—and Simon decided to give a great feast in Jesus' honor to thank Him. Although Simon was grateful and impressed with Jesus' power in healing, Simon had not accepted Jesus as the Messiah. And he had never admitted any guilt for the way he had treated Mary.

Knowing the kind of man Simon was, why did Jesus heal him?
Why do you think Jesus accepted Simon's invitation to dinner?

Simon invited the most important people in Bethany to the feast. Lazarus, whom Jesus had raised from the dead, Martha, Jesus and His disciples, and many others were there. Mary was also there, trying not to be noticed, but wanting to be near enough to Jesus to hear every word He said.

Mary had a small alabaster box hidden in the folds of her robe. She had sacrificed a great deal to be able to buy it. Hearing Jesus say He was going to die, Mary bought the perfume as a way of showing Him honor in death. Now, however, she heard people talking about crowning Him King, and she was eager to be the first to honor Him in life. Moving close to where He was sitting, Mary broke open the box and poured the perfume on His head and His feet. As she knelt before Him, her joy spilling over in tears, Mary wiped His feet with her long, flowing hair.

Mary had hoped no one would notice, but the fragrance of the perfume filled the room, and everyone soon knew what she had done. Imagine Judas saying, "Did you ever see anything so disgusting? What a waste! We could have traded the perfume for money, lots of it! Think of the food it would have bought for poor people here in Bethany." Other guests criticized her just as harshly.

Mary was embarrassed as the murmurs of disapproval filled the room. She had forgotten herself completely. To her it was as if Jesus were the only One present.

Then Jesus came to her rescue. "'Why criticize this woman for doing such a good thing to me? You will always have the poor among you, but you will not always have me. She has poured this perfume on me to prepare my body for burial. I tell you the truth, wherever the Good News is preached through-out the world, this woman's deed will be remembered and discussed'" (Matthew 26:10–13).

Simon had seen what had happened and heard what Jesus said, although he pretended not to notice. He was irritated by the way Jesus treated Mary, whom he despised. He thought to himself, "'If this man were a prophet, he would know what kind of woman is touching him. She's a sinner!'" (Luke 7:39). He did not recognize that he had as great a need to be forgiven as did Mary.

Jesus knew what Simon was thinking. Turning toward him, Jesus said, "'Simon, I have something to say to you'" (Luke 7:40). Can you imagine how Simon must have felt? No doubt he had heard that Jesus seemed to be able to read people's minds, and perhaps he wondered if Jesus would humili-ate him in front of everyone. He could already imagine the gossip that would spread through Bethany the next day. As Simon began to feel pain and embarrassment, Jesus simply told a story that only Simon could understand. It was a parable about two men who owed a third man money. One of them owed five hundred days' wages. The other owed fifty. The trouble was that neither man could pay his debt. The parable ended happily, however, because the man to whom they owed the money canceled both debts.

"'Who do you suppose loved him more after that?'" Jesus asked.

"Simon answered, 'I suppose the one for whom he canceled the larger debt'" (Luke 7:42, 43).

"'That's right.'" Jesus looked at Mary and then at Simon. "'Look at this woman kneeling here. When I entered your home, you didn't offer me water to wash the dust from my feet, but she has washed them with her tears and wiped them with her hair. You didn't greet me with a kiss, but from the time I first came in, she has not stopped kissing my feet. You neglected the courtesy of olive oil to anoint my head, but she has anointed my feet with rare perfume'" (Luke 7:43–46). Jesus tactfully pointed out the many opportunities Simon had to show his appreciation for what Jesus had done for him. Simon thought that he had honored Jesus by inviting Him to his house. Now he realized that Jesus had honored him, instead.

It was then that Simon saw himself as he really was, a proud, guilty man. Simon realized that Jesus was not going to treat him as he had wanted Mary to be treated. Jesus was not going to expose his guilt to others or condemn him openly for what he had done. The way Jesus treated him led Simon to repentance and changed his whole life. He became a humble follower of the Savior.

? **What did Jesus do that showed that He loved Simon too?**

In the tragic days that followed, Mary kept as close to Jesus as she dared. She stood at the foot of the cross to be near Him during His hours of suffering.

After Jesus' death, Mary followed His body to the tomb and lingered there when all the others had gone. She was the first at the tomb early on Sunday morning. There she saw, through her tears, Someone she thought was the gardener. But the Gardener was Jesus! Alive!

As soon as Jesus spoke her name, Mary knew Him. From among all His friends and followers, Jesus chose to first reveal Himself to Mary.

Mary, the woman who knew she was a sinner, was now chosen by Christ to carry the news that He was alive to His sorrowing disciples.

GETTING TO KNOW GOD

Journal

- Perhaps the Holy Spirit is gently telling you that you need to ask for forgiveness in your life. Write about a change you would like to make; then pray for the power of the Holy Spirit to help you make the change.

Dig a Little Deeper

1. In this lesson you have read about two people whose lives were greatly changed because of the way Jesus treated them. Describe what Jesus did for each of them that caused them to change.

2. Some important things about sin, confession, and forgiveness are found in the following verses. Explain what God will do for us when we confess our sins. What should we do if someone wrongs us? 1 John 1:5–10; Matthew 6:14, 15; 18:21, 22

3. Jesus forgave Mary each time she sinned and asked for forgiveness.
   a. What must we do before God can forgive us? Psalms 66:18; 86:5
   b. Name at least one other Bible story that demonstrates God's forgiveness.
   c. Could there be a sin that Jesus does not forgive? Matthew 12:31, 32

4. Mary's gift cost her a great deal of money, but something other than money made it even more valuable to Jesus. What do you think it was?
   "The fragrant gift which Mary had thought to lavish upon the dead body of the Saviour she poured upon His living form. At the burial its sweetness could only have pervaded the tomb; now it gladdened His heart with the assurance of her faith and love. . . . The women who bore spices to the tomb found their errand in vain, for He had risen. But Mary, pouring out her love upon the Saviour while He was conscious of her devotion, was anointing Him for the burial. And as He went down into the darkness of His great trial, He carried with Him the memory of that deed, an earnest [token] of the love that would be His from His redeemed ones forever" (*The Desire of Ages*, p. 560).

5. Like Mary, we sometimes have to make "how much" decisions. For example: How much shall I give for offering? How much shall I do to help my neighbor?
   a. Think of at least two other examples of "how much" decisions you or your friends might have to make.
   b. A "how much" decision is often difficult. If a person decides to give only the smallest amount possible, what is he saying about him- or herself? What does this action say about his or her professed love for God?

Activities

A. Design and construct an attractive box to remind you of Mary's alabaster box. Use it as a container for a collection of Bible verses and/or quotations that tell you something about the way Jesus treats people.

B. Prepare a monologue. Imagine that you are Lazarus, Mary, Martha, Simon, or Judas; verbalize the thoughts of the character chosen.
   • What is the most important thing to you?
   • What is your attitude toward Jesus?
   • What are the feelings or emotions that you had when you saw what Mary did and the response of the people?
   Present your monologue to another class or at an assembly.

C. Mary's gift was beautiful, not only because it was costly, but because in giving the gift she was motivated by love and gratitude. Today we can show our love for Jesus by giving the gift of service to others. Matthew 25:40 tells how important this gift is to Jesus. As a class make a plan to help someone and then do it! Here are some ideas:
   1. Help a younger child at school.
   2. Develop a worship program and present it to your class, school, or church.
   3. Help a neighbor with chores.
   4. Spend time with someone who is lonely.

D. Mary's witness was symbolic when she washed Jesus' feet at Simon's house. Use *The Desire of Ages*, chapter 62, pp. 560–566 to find what the following acts symbolize:
   1. The great value of the gift, perhaps Mary's life savings
   2. The broken alabaster box
   3. The perfume/ointment
   4. The fragrance that filled the whole room
   5. The unselfish love that prompted so great a gift

To Learn More

The Bible Pageant (1986), vol. 4, pp. 83, 84
The Bible Story, vol. 9, pp. 28–32, 151–155
The Desire of Ages, chap. 62
Messiah, chap. 62

15

GETTING TO KNOW GOD

"See how very much our Father loves us, for he calls us his children, and that is what we are! But the people who belong to this world don't recognize that we are God's children because they don't know him. Dear friends, we are already God's children, but he has not yet shown us what we will be like when Christ appears. But we do know that we will be like him, for we will see him as he really is" (1 John 3:1, 2).

Change, who can change? Can you? "This is the way I am, like it or not." Or maybe you say, "My parents are responsible for the way I act. They are the ones to blame. Don't blame me!" Have you ever heard these remarks made by people giving excuses for their behavior? Who is to blame for how we are? Genes we inherit from our parents? The neighborhood in which we live? The school we attend? Our friends? Guess again.

The Power of Love

John 12:35, 36

John was a young fisherman—proud, ambitious, bad tempered, and critical. He and his brother, James, were called the sons of thunder! All this changed when John met Jesus. One of the first invited to join Jesus as He traveled around Palestine, John observed Jesus, and a strong desire to become like Him grew. He stayed near the Savior and yielded himself to the power of that perfect life and its example.

The Scripture states: "Whenever someone turns to the Lord, the veil is taken away. . . . So all of us who have had that veil removed can see and reflect the glory of the Lord. And the Lord—who is the Spirit—makes us more and more like him as we are changed into his glorious image" (2 Corinthians 3:16–18). The more John watched and listened to Jesus, the more his respect and love for the Savior grew. Gradually his character was reshaped to become like Jesus. He learned that Jesus was truly his Friend. Even when John failed, Jesus did not stop loving him. John made the decision that above all, he wanted to be like this Man he loved. That's what changed him, Jesus' great love for him. It gave him strength, determination, and confidence.

Is there someone you love and admire who encourages you to change?

Old habits and attitudes do not change easily. John still wanted to be first in everything. Once his mother asked Jesus if her two sons, James and John, could occupy high positions in His kingdom. Jesus knew the motive behind her question and focused on the need for character development. A position in the kingdom is not given to favorites; is not earned or bestowed. "It is the result of character. The crown and the throne are the tokens of a condition attained—tokens of self-conquest through the grace of our Lord Jesus Christ" (*The Acts of the Apostles,* p. 543).

GETTING TO KNOW GOD

At a time of Jesus' greatest need, He asked John, along with James and Peter, to stay nearby as He prayed in the Garden of Gethsemane. This was the night of His betrayal. "My soul is crushed with grief to the point of death. Stay here and keep watch with me" (Matthew 26:38). Jesus went a little farther into the Garden alone and knelt to pray. He came back to the three disciples, wanting assurance and comfort. He found that John, who claimed to be Jesus' dearest friend, along with the others, was sleeping. The One who had demonstrated such firmness against opposition now was being buffeted and bent by the mighty weight of the sin of all humankind.

? *Can you think of a time when you felt alone and deserted?*

Twice Jesus returned to find the disciples sleeping. Hearing His voice, they roused but were again overcome by sleep and paid little attention to the needs of their Master. Then, when the soldiers and mob came to arrest Jesus, John was afraid and ran away.

Though he failed Jesus in the Garden, John could not stay away from his Friend. Jesus' love drew him back. John was there at Jesus' trial. When Jesus was mocked and beaten, John was with Him. When Jesus suffered on the cross, John was there, caring for Jesus' mother. On Sunday morning, John was one of the first at the tomb.

John's life was changed by witnessing the patience Jesus displayed during His suffering and trial. John's life was changed by personally experiencing the love and forgiveness of Jesus. Later, when John was arrested by the religious leaders for preaching the news of Jesus' resurrection, he courageously responded, "Do you think God wants us to obey you rather than him? We cannot stop telling about everything we have seen and heard" (Acts 4:19, 20). John's experience had been too overwhelming, and he was unable to deny that which he knew to be true. Each day John's heart was open to Jesus. His love of self was completely overwhelmed by the love he had for his Master.

This same John who had wanted to call down fire from heaven to destroy a Samaritan village which showed no hospitality to Jesus was now one of the first to demonstrate the loving forgiveness he had experienced. This same John who had been a son of thunder was now identified as the disciple Jesus loved. He was ready to write of the birth of the Son of God and of the sinless life He lived. John was a living testimony of the love of His Maker, Friend, and Redeemer.

The Gospel written by John is known as a book of stories in which Jesus demonstrates God's love. John's letters to the church stress the need for this transformation. His experiences enabled him to write personally of that which he had seen and learned by following in his Master's steps.

John's life was a constant testimony for Christ. His wisdom, eloquence, and power spoke of unfathomable love, and his life and writings bore testimony of all that he knew. Ever present were those who would deny his truths, those who, from the beginning, wrestled against powers of heaven. Though placed into a caldron of boiling oil, John was protected as were the three Hebrews in the fiery furnace on the plains of Dura. Though banished to a rocky inhospitable island, John was drawn closer to nature and to its Creator. Writing of the visions given by God during this time, John's words are recorded in the last book of the Bible, Revelation.

What do you do when adversity comes?

Many of us are much like John. We have strong points and weak ones. We stand up bravely at times and are careless, rebellious, or frightened at other times. But, like John, we, too, can grow to be more and more like Jesus. How? In much the same way that John did. John saw Jesus in person and stayed close to Him. We can see Jesus by reading the stories of the Bible and by thinking of what they tell us about Him.

The promise Jesus made to send the Holy Spirit after He returned to heaven was fulfilled. In reading about Jesus, we learn to love and trust Him. As we choose to obey Him, we can be changed to reflect His likeness through the gift of the Holy Spirit. While John was able to talk with Him, face to face, we can talk to Him in prayer. We can depend on Him and His promise. We can be open and receptive to what He tells us. We can speak for Him.

The God we worship changes us through the Holy Spirit from all we wish we were not to all He wants us to be.

GETTING TO KNOW GOD

Journal

- What habits and attitudes do you have that might need to be changed?

- What habits and attitudes would you like to establish that would help you to know Jesus better?

Dig a Little Deeper

1. John wrote about the divinity of Jesus. He provided clear testimony and evidence that Jesus was fully human and fully God. Read John 1:1–5 and answer the following questions.
   a. Who was the Word?
   b. With whom did the Word exist?
   c. Who was the Creator?
   d. What did the Word do?

2. Was John immediately changed into a different kind of person by his association with Jesus? Give examples to explain your answer.

3. Jesus had the power to change John, but what was the one thing John had to do for himself?

4. Using the narrative for your answers, list three ways in which John was changed.

5. In the books that John wrote, he quoted Jesus many times. Make a note of the main idea in each of the following texts. Use your notes to compose a short paragraph describing the big idea or theme that runs through all of them. John 15:12; 1 John 3:1; 1 John 4:20, 21; 2 John 6

6. When you read stories of Jesus in the Bible, often John is not far away. In the Gospel John wrote, he calls himself "another disciple." Tell where John was on each occasion described in the following texts: John 18:15; John 19:25–27; John 20:2–8; John 21:2–7.

Activities

A. After reading John 15:12 and 1 John 4:20, 21, make a greeting card that expresses appreciation to someone who has shown you this same type of loving kindness that Jesus showed to John.

B. Think about the friends in your life. Write a paragraph describing how your life has been influenced in a positive way by one or several of these friends.

C. Research the name *Philadelphia*. What does it mean? How could your community or school earn such a name?

D. Use a concordance to locate verses that mention John the disciple. List ten or more texts and explain what is said about John in each text. (Example: John 18:15: John follows Jesus into the court of the high priest.)

To Learn More

The Acts of the Apostles, pp. 546–556, 568–577, 581–592

Memory Verse

"They said to each other, 'Didn't our hearts burn within us as he talked with us on the road and explained the Scriptures to us?'" (Luke 24:32).

Feeling lonely and disappointed, the two weary travelers trudged along the road from Jerusalem to Emmaus one Sunday afternoon, a long, long time ago. Their discouragement seemed overwhelming. They wondered why God let such a thing happen.

"Stay With Us"

Luke 24:13–35

Readers:	**Narrator 1, Narrator 2, Narrator 3, Narrator 4, Narrator 5, Narrator 6, Narrator 7, Cleopas, Companion, Jesus**

Narrator 1: Two of Jesus' followers plod along the road that winds from Jerusalem to the little town of Emmaus. Their drooping shoulders and weary gait reflect the hopelessness they feel.

Cleopas: Why? Why did it have to happen this way? I will never understand it. Passover is supposed to be a time to celebrate. Instead, we are mourning.

Companion: I feel the same way. It's like some terrible confusing dream. Just a few days ago He came into the city, remember? The people treated Him like a king. When they shouted, "Hosanna" and waved palm branches, I was so sure that He was finally going to free us from the Romans.

Narrator 2: The road stretches out before them, dry and dusty and lonely. Soon a traveler catches up with them.

Jesus: You two look so sad. What is really bothering you? Why are you so sad?

Companion: You must be the only person in Jerusalem who hasn't heard about it.

Jesus: Heard about what?

Cleopas:	The terrible things that happened to Jesus, the Carpenter from Nazareth. He was a prophet and mighty teacher. He was always performing miracles and healing people. We thought He was the Messiah who would save us from the Romans. But now He is dead. I knew the religious leaders hated Him, but they actually had Him killed.
Jesus:	Tell me more about it.
Companion:	This morning some women from our group, followers of His, went out to the tomb. They found it open and His body missing. They say they saw two angels who told them Jesus is alive!
Cleopas:	Friends of ours went to see for themselves, and they were right—Jesus' body was gone. We heard a rumor that it had been stolen during the night. So many strange things are going on. It's all so confusing. Anyway, we are going home.
Jesus:	Why does this trouble you so much? Why is it so hard to believe what the prophets wrote in the Scriptures? Don't you know that the Christ had to suffer these things and then would enter into His glory?
Narrator 1:	It's a seven-mile trip from Jerusalem to Emmaus. All the way the Stranger talks with them. Beginning with Moses, He reviews the Old Testament stories and prophecies about the Messiah.
Narrator 2:	These prophecies told of His coming, His life on earth, His suffering and death. The Stranger doesn't want these two discouraged people to think that He is the Messiah just because He says so. He wants them to believe because the Scriptures are filled with the evidence that what He is telling them is the truth.

Narrator 3:	Imagine the thoughts going through the minds of those who followed Jesus. *Is this what was supposed to happen to the Messiah? Is this what the prophets were telling us?* Cleopas and his companion must have thought to themselves, *This is just the way Jesus would talk.*
Narrator 4:	As they near Emmaus, their conversation with the Stranger comes to an end.
Companion:	We live right over there.
Narrator 3:	As the Stranger begins to move on down the road, Cleopas and his companion realize how much they want Him to stay.
Cleopas:	Will you stay with us? The day is almost gone. Soon it will be dark. Come and have dinner with us.
Narrator 4:	At first the Stranger seems to hesitate, but then accepts their invitation. The simple meal is prepared and placed before their Guest, who is seated at the head of the table. When He puts out His hands to bless the food, the two stare incredulously. He did that exactly the way they had seen Jesus do.
Narrator 5:	He reaches out, takes a small loaf of bread, and breaks it. It was then that they noticed His scarred hands.
Cleopas:	He is Jesus!
Companion:	Lord!
Narrator 5:	And He was gone. The two look at each other in amazement.
Cleopas:	They were right about the tomb! Jesus is alive! He really is the Messiah! We shouldn't have been so confused when He died. It happened just as the Scriptures said it would!

Companion:	We've got to tell the others!
Narrator 6:	Cleopas and his companion jump up from the table. They take off running toward Jerusalem. Forgetting how tired and hungry they are, they cover those seven miles faster than ever before.
Narrator 7:	Can't you just see them pounding on the locked door of the upper room? One of the disciples cautiously opens the door—just a bit. Just enough for the two from Emmaus to shout their thrilling news. Eleven frightened men soon rejoice with hope and excitement.
Narrator 6:	As Cleopas and his companion enter the room, an unseen Visitor enters with them. When Jesus appears to them, it is a powerful scene.
Narrator 7:	Just as Jesus revealed Himself to the believers, He will always reveal Himself to those with open and receptive hearts.

GETTING TO KNOW GOD

Journal

- What might have been the clue for you that the Stranger walking with you was Jesus? Explain.

Dig a Little Deeper

1. List two things that helped convince Cleopas and his companion that Jesus was the Messiah.

2. The invitation given to Jesus is an important part of the experience in this story. Read what Ellen White said about the invitation and answer the questions that follow.

   "Had the disciples failed to press their invitation, they would not have known that their traveling companion was the risen Lord. Christ never forces His company upon anyone. He interests Himself in those who need Him. Gladly will He enter the humblest home, and cheer the lowliest heart. But if men are too indifferent to think of the heavenly Guest, or ask Him to abide with them, He passes on. Thus many meet with great loss. They do not know Christ any more than did the disciples as He walked with them by the way" (*The Desire of Ages*, p. 800).

   a. What do you think "press their invitation" means? Use a dictionary if necessary.
   b. Why was it important for Cleopas and his companion to press their invitation?
   c. According to the paragraph above, what can a person do to really know Christ?
   d. Why does Christ never force Himself upon anyone?

3. How can we be sure that we do not have the same misunderstanding as the two disciples walking to Emmaus? John 14:26; Acts 17:11

4. John 4:5–30 and 39–42 tell how some other people reacted when they had been in the presence of the Messiah. Who were they? How did they react?

5. Paul listed certain facts about Jesus, beginning with "Christ died for our sins." After reading 1 Corinthians 15:3–8, explain in your own words at least five other things Paul said about Jesus. Why do you think Paul stated all of these facts about Jesus?

6. According to Paul, how important is the fact that Jesus was raised from the dead? 1 Corinthians 15:14. Tell how important this is to you.

Activities

A. Imagine you were a reporter for the *Jerusalem Times*. Write a news article describing an interview you have just had with Cleopas either Sunday morning or after his return to Jerusalem from Emmaus.
OR
Write an editorial telling how, after the current news, you are being convinced that Jesus is really the Messiah.

B. Make a calculated guess as to how long it would take to slowly walk seven miles. Compare the time it would take to run seven miles. You may wish to use your school track to make your estimations. How long could it have taken Cleopas and his companion to walk when they were discouraged? How fast could they have made the trip after they met Jesus? What made the difference?

C. Draw a picture of one of the following:
   1. Two disciples and Jesus walking to Emmaus.
   2. The surprised look on the disciples' faces as they recognize Jesus at the supper table.

D. Divide a large sheet of paper or poster board into three columns. In a cooperative group, brainstorm evidence that God gives us today of His presence. In another column, list reasons we can be unaware of this evidence. In a third column, find passages of Scripture that would encourage you to become more aware of God's presence.

To Learn More

The Bible Pageant (1986), vol. 4, pp. 166–168
The Bible Story, vol. 9, pp. 156–164
The Desire of Ages, chaps. 84; 85
Messiah, chaps. 84; 85

God's plan for you is beautiful and complete, and it involves every aspect of your life. Daily you are faced with decisions. Choose to become like Him.

unit 4

CHOOSING GOD

While You're Studying

A Write the memory verses for the unit and add them to your file.

B Create a booklet or PowerPoint® presentation for younger children showing the eight principles of health.

C Make an appointment with God. Design a calendar for the month. Be creative as you plan prayer and study time for each day. Think of what you might study and where you will spend your quiet time with God.

D As a culminating activity for the unit, publish a newspaper covering the topics that were studied. Your paper could include feature articles about each of the lessons, artwork, an advice column, letters to the editor, photos, an editorial, or poetry.

© DARREL TANK

17

CHOOSING GOD

Memory Verse

"You will receive power when the Holy Spirit comes upon you. And you will be my witnesses, telling people about me everywhere—in Jerusalem, throughout Judea, in Samaria, and to the ends of the earth" (Acts 1:8).

"You will be my witnesses . . . to the ends of the earth" are the words Jesus used when He called the disciples to witness about His life and death and resurrection. In the same way, He calls you today to witness about His love and saving power.

The Gospel According to You

Matthew 28:18–20

Jesus is speaking with His disciples on the Mount of Olives, just outside Jerusalem. Soon He will disappear from their sight, but He lingers to talk with them. These men who had become His close friends during those three years of ministry were the very ones who would be sharing His message with the world. Can you imagine Jesus looking at them and calling them by name? "You, John, James, Andrew, Philip, Thomas, Bartholomew, Peter, Thaddaeus, and Matthew, and you, James, the son of Alphaeus, and Simon, each of you, all of you, will be My witnesses. Tell everyone everywhere what you have seen and heard about Me. And no matter what, I will always be with you."

The time these men had spent with Jesus had changed them. Ellen G. White describes this transformation:

> "Under the training of Christ the disciples had been led to feel their need of the Spirit. Under the Spirit's teaching they received the final qualification, and went forth to their lifework. No longer were they ignorant and uncultured. No longer were they a collection of independent units or discordant, conflicting elements. No longer were their hopes set on worldly greatness. They were of 'one accord,' 'of one heart and of one soul' Acts 2:46; 4:32" (*The Acts of the Apostles*, p. 45).

The Master knew He could depend on His friends, and they did not fail Him. They went first to Jerusalem, then all over the world carrying the good news. Not only did they preach about Jesus, they represented Him by the way they treated people. They told about Him by the way they acted when others treated them in a cruel or unkind manner.

The belief and confidence in God that the apostles possessed spoke of the power of a risen Christ. After Peter healed a crippled beggar, he and John were arrested and put in jail. The next day they appeared before the members of the council in Jerusalem. "The members of the council were amazed when they saw the boldness of Peter and John, for they could see that they were ordinary men with no special training in the Scriptures. They also recognized them as men who had been with Jesus" (Acts 4:13). God was using ordinary men with ordinary abilities to do extraordinary things.

Two thousand years later, Christ continues to call disciples. He asks you to represent Him. He calls you in much the same way He called His disciples by saying, "Come, follow me, and I will show you how to fish for people!" (Matthew 4:19). He doesn't ask you to live as the disciples lived or to work in the same way they worked. He asks you to do something that only you can do. It may be difficult to believe, but Christ has an opportunity to witness that is a custom-fit for you. His plan includes representing Him right now where you are.

Being God's witness will involve every part of your existence. It will affect the way you relate to others, the way you think and talk, the way you play, the way you decide what is important in your life.

Much of Jesus' life on earth was spent working in Nazareth, where He worked in a carpenter shop. As He lived in that community, his family and his neighbors did not know that He was the Son of God. But Jesus was doing His Father's work just as much when He worked as a carpenter as when He was healing the sick or calming the stormy waves of Galilee. Serving Jesus happens as we go about the humble duties of our lives.

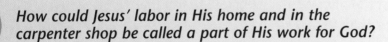

? *How could Jesus' labor in His home and in the carpenter shop be called a part of His work for God?*

Many people miss the opportunity to be a tremendous witness for God because they feel that their contributions are so small, they are unqualified, or there are so many others who could do a more effective job. But witnessing for Jesus is a job for everyone, not just those who seem to be well qualified. Think for a moment about a pool of water that is very still. When one throws a pebble in, the ripples begin to spread. They circle on and on.

The words and actions of those who love God can have a far-reaching effect in the lives of those around them. Many will never know they have had such influence until they reach heaven. Then they will learn that their daily lives, their sincere faith, was a testimony that led others to God (adapted from *Steps to Christ,* pp. 82, 83).

? *How does being a witness for Jesus affect the way one does daily chores? The way one does schoolwork?*

We hear the names of some of Jesus' disciples more than others. Take Andrew, for example. Little is said about him in the Gospels. When we first meet Andrew, he is with John the Baptist, out near the Jordan River. He has listened to John telling people the Messiah has come to earth, and he is eager to know more about Him. Now as Andrew and one of his friends are talking with John, they notice he is not looking at them. His eyes are on Someone he sees in the crowd.

"Look!" John cries. Andrew and his friend turn to look at the young Man at whom John is pointing. *Can He be the Messiah,* they wonder? In awe and silence they hurry after Him, at first saying nothing. Then one of them asks, "Where do You live?" and Jesus replies, "Come and see." That is all the invitation they need. They spend the rest of the day together with Jesus. What a day!

Andrew is so excited about what Jesus has told him that he simply cannot keep it to himself. As soon as he can, Andrew goes to find his brother, Peter.

"Peter, I have found the Messiah! He told me wonderful things, but it wasn't just the things He said; it was the way He said them. Come with me. You must meet Him."

Peter, too, had heard John the Baptist explain the prophecies about the Messiah. He realized that something had happened to his brother, and he was curious. By going with Andrew to meet Jesus, Peter's life was never the same again.

Before that day, both Peter and Andrew had spent their lives fishing. When Jesus stood on the shore near where they were working and called, "Follow Me," they gladly left their nets and their boat to be with Him.

In quiet everyday ways, Andrew was a witness for the Savior. Imagine Jesus saying to Andrew, "Well done, my good and faithful servant. You have been faithful in handling this small amount, so now I will give you many more responsibilities. Let's celebrate together!" (Matthew 25:21).

Andrew and his brother, Peter, came from a life of poverty, while Matthew came from one of wealth. Yet, all were witnesses for Jesus. It doesn't matter where people come from, how much wealth they possess, or how powerful they are. What does make the difference is the desire to do what God wants one to do, to want others to have the opportunity to know Him. He can use you as a witness for Him.

Do you remember the story of the time Jesus and His disciples visited Garasenes (or Gadarenes in some translations)? Two men had terrorized the entire countryside for years. They looked and acted more like fierce animals than men, and the disciples fled in fear when they appeared. But not Jesus. He looked at them with pity, held up His hand, and stopped them as they dashed toward

CHOOSING GOD

Him. Then, with just a word, Jesus healed them. Suddenly the wild men's minds were clear, and they were able to understand what Jesus had done for them. Imagine their feelings of freedom and joy! Soon, clothed and with clear minds, they were sitting at His feet, listening, understanding, and accepting

what He was telling them. They were so overwhelmed as Jesus left that they begged Him to let them go along.

But Jesus had other plans for the two men. He said, "No, go home to your family, and tell them everything the Lord has done for you and how merciful he has been" (Mark 5:19). They had listened to Jesus for only a little while. In spite of the fact they had never heard one of His sermons, they had been changed. Jesus had a special work for them that only they could do. That special work was to show their families and their neighbors what Jesus had done for them.

The greatest place to be a witness is right where you are—at home, at school, at church, or in your neighborhood. When Jesus calls you to wider fields, you will be ready because you have learned to say through your actions and attitudes, "Let me tell you about my Friend, Jesus!"

CHOOSING GOD

Journal

- What are some ways you can represent Christ?

Dig a Little Deeper

1. Define *witness.* Use a dictionary or a thesaurus.

2. Name three ways in which the disciples were witnesses for God.

3. After reading Matthew 25:14, 20, 21, Ecclesiastes 9:10, and the passage below, list at least three ways you can develop your witness for God.

   > Talents grow as they are used. Success is not the result of chance: It is the reward of faith, of wise choices, and of determined effort. The Lord wants us to use every gift He has given us, and if we do this, we shall have greater gifts to use.
   >
   > Every effort made for Christ will react in blessings upon ourselves. If we use our abilities for His glory, He will give us more (adapted from *Christ's Object Lessons,* pp. 353, 354).

4. Even though what you do is a witness to God and His love, there are times when it is important to talk to a person directly about Jesus. Peter has some suggestions for doing this.

   > "You must worship Christ as Lord of your life. And if someone asks about your Christian hope, always be ready to explain it. But do this in a gentle and respectful way. Keep your conscience clear. Then if people speak against you, they will be ashamed when they see what a good life you live because you belong to Christ" (1 Peter 3:15, 16).

   a. What does Peter say you should do before you talk to someone about Jesus?
   b. What does Peter say about the way in which you should talk to your questioner?
   c. Why do you think the way you answer him is important?

5. Paul wrote to friends in Corinth about being a living letter (2 Corinthians 3:2, 3). Ellen White writes of living letters too.

   > "In every one of His children, Jesus sends a letter to the world. If you are Christ's follower, He sends in you a letter to the family, the village, the street, where you live. Jesus, dwelling in you, desires to speak to the hearts of those who are not acquainted with Him. Perhaps they do not read the Bible, or do not hear the voice that speaks to them in its pages; they do not see the love of God through His works. But if you are a true representative of Jesus, it may be that through you they will be led to understand something of His goodness and be won to love and serve Him" (*Steps to Christ,* p. 115).

   a. What do you think it means to be "a letter from Christ"?
   b. Identify two ways you can be such a letter.

Activities

A.   People often judge the entire Seventh-day Adventist Church by the everyday lives of its members. Good witnesses recognize the importance of unselfishness, carefulness, and honesty both in word and action. Write a skit about something your church does for mission outreach or about being an effective witness and present it to the class.

B.   Using the letters of your first name, make an acrostic telling ways in which you might be a message for God.

C.   Divide your class into groups. Have each group choose one of the situations described. For the situation selected, answer the following questions:
1. What could you do to be witnesses for Jesus?
2. What characteristics of Jesus would your actions reveal?
3. What abilities, talents, or skills are needed to be witnesses for God in this situation?

Situation 1: A classmate has been ill for more than a week and is far behind in his math assignments. Your class is too large for your teacher to be able to spend much time with him.

Situation 2: Your class learns that during a recent storm, a large tree has fallen into the yard of an elderly widow. She has no one to help her clean up the fallen limbs.

Situation 3: There is a large patch of bare land, often strewn with litter, near your school. It is not fenced in or otherwise restricted.

Situation 4: Recesses or intramurals have become the scene of constant arguing. Winning has become all-important.

D.   Work with your teacher to form a "greeting committee" of interested students to welcome people to Sabbath School.
1. Make arrangements with the Sabbath School superintendent.
2. Be well-groomed and dressed neatly.
3. Practice in class how to greet church members and guests.

To Learn More

The Desire of Ages, chap. 14
Messiah, chap. 14
The Bible Pageant (1986), vol. 4, pp. 47, 48, 90, 91, 169–173
The Bible Story, vol. 7, pp. 122–124; vol. 9, pp. 184, 185

18

CHOOSING GOD

Memory Verse

"Don't copy the behavior and customs of this world, but let God transform you into a new person by changing the way you think. Then you will learn to know God's will for you, which is good and pleasing and perfect" (Romans 12:2).

Your life is a reflection of all the choices you make. What you allow into your mind affects all aspects of your life. Just as the food you take into your body promotes either good or bad physical health, the books you read, the music you listen to, the TV programs you watch, the thoughts you cherish will be reflected in your attitudes and actions. What will your choice be?

What Makes You "You"?

Psalm 139:14

The mind is the one thing that makes each person unique. From the mind come thoughts, hopes, memories, decisions, and actions. What your mind is, you are. There is no other person exactly like you in the whole world.

Senses are the doorways to the mind. The mind can combine the bits of information given by the senses in an endless number of ways. That is why you can think very complicated thoughts, why you know so much already, why you can imagine things, and why you will learn so much more as you continue to think and grow. No wonder the Bible says you are "wonderfully complex" (Psalm 139:14).

The war for control of your mind began before this earth was created. There is a life-and-death struggle between good and evil. Satan is seeking to destroy all. However, "No man without his own consent can be overcome by Satan. The tempter has no power to control the will or to force the soul to sin" (*The Great Controversy,* p. 510).

> *Is it possible to remain neutral when both God and the world are trying to gain access to our minds?*

God has given you a mind with power to think and with freedom to make your own choices. The quality of your life is determined by how you use this freedom. God counsels you to guard the doorways to your mind. What you see, hear, read, where you go, how you choose your friends, and what you eat or drink will affect you and your relationships with your family and with God.

> *Does God force us to follow His instructions and counsel? Can the devil force us to follow his?*

Gradually your mind adapts to what you spend a great deal of time

CHOOSING GOD

thinking about, listening to, looking at, and doing. Thoughts that are repeated become a way of thinking. Actions follow thoughts, and actions that are repeated become habits. This is what Paul meant when he wrote, "Don't copy the behavior and customs of this world, but let God transform you into a new person by changing the way you think. Then you will learn to know God's will for you, which is good and pleasing and perfect" (Romans 12:2).

One way to guard the doorways to your mind is to read the Bible thoughtfully. As you do, the Holy Spirit will guide you to greater understanding. The more you study, the more you will understand and the easier it will be for you to make wise choices.

Another way to guard the doorways to your mind is by prayer. Ask God to give you a clear mind. Be willing to listen to what He says. Tell Him that you want to be obedient to Him. "Prayer is the opening of the heart to God as to a friend. Not that it is necessary in order to make known to God what we are, but in order to enable us to receive Him. Prayer does not bring God down to us, but brings us up to Him" (*Steps to Christ,* p. 93).

The Holy Spirit also impresses upon you ways to guard the doorways to your mind. His still, small voice can lead you to choices that are best for you. By listening to the Holy Spirit, you will become more like Jesus. "Letting the Spirit control your mind leads to life and peace" (Romans 8:6).

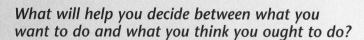

What will help you decide between what you want to do and what you think you ought to do?

Every action you take begins with a choice. Choosing not to let anything enter your mind that separates you from God is an important decision. As you cooperate with God, you will gain strength to become like Him.

As you make choices, ask yourself questions like these:
1. Why do I want to do this?
2. Will it violate any of God's laws?
3. What kind of influence will my decision have on myself and on others?
4. Am I willing to listen to what God has to tell me?
5. Am I willing to follow God's instructions?

Prayerfully ask God to help you with your decisions. Surrender your will to God, inviting Him to be in charge of your life.

God made you, and He wants you to be the best "you" you can be. When you fill your mind with good things, you crowd out worthless things. "Fix your thoughts on what is true, and honorable, and right, and pure, and lovely, and admirable. Think about things that are excellent and worthy of praise" (Philippians 4:8).

CHOOSING GOD

Journal

- What will help you decide between what you want to do and what you think you ought to do?

Dig a Little Deeper

1. Paul and Peter both talk about struggling about doing what is right.
   a. With whom did Paul say that we struggle? Ephesians 6:12
   b. What warning did Peter give? 1 Peter 5:8

2. Write the key idea in each of these texts that explains how the war for control of your mind can be won. 1 John 5:4; Philippians 2:5; Psalm 119:11

3. Other Bible writers have some advice about responding to all the information that is shouting for your attention. Put the key phrases in your own words. Psalm 19:14; 1 Peter 3:10, 11; Isaiah 26:3; Proverbs 4:23–25

4. Ellen White said, "Everything depends on the right action of the will" (*Steps to Christ,* p. 47). What would you say is the right action of the will for those who want to make the best use of the marvelous mind God has given them? Joshua 24:14, 15

5. Each of the following verses from Philippians 4 helps to explain something you can do as your part of God's plan. Read the verse first; then rewrite the main idea in your own words.
   a. Philippians 4:4
   b. Philippians 4:5
   c. Philippians 4:6
   d. Philippians 4:8
   e. Philippians 4:11

Activities

A. Write a poem. Choose one of the following topics.
    1. What makes you, "you"?
    2. Making positive choices

B. Divide the class into five groups. Have each group choose ways to guard one of the five senses. Present your findings to the class. Your presentations could be in the form of skits, role playing, PowerPoint® illustrations, songs, or posters.

C. Plan a social event for your class that would reflect positive choices.

D. Construct a diagram that shows how positive choices help us to have healthy minds.

To Learn More

Education, chap. 13
Steps to Jesus, chaps. 8; 10

Memory Verse

"Whether you eat or drink, or whatever you do, do it all for the glory of God" (1 Corinthians 10:31).

There are eight principles of health that can lead to both a healthy body and a healthy mind: Fresh air, sunlight, sobriety*, rest, exercise, proper diet, water, and trust in divine power—these are the true remedies.

*abstemiousness

The Healthy Christian

1 Corinthians 6:19, 20

Living on an academy campus, the elementary students enjoyed being visited by Week of Prayer speakers when they came to meet with academy students. This week was a little different. It was student Week of Prayer, and academy students were studying how to relate to the world around them, how to develop empathy for those who barely subsist in our world, how to be like Jesus. They had the option of living a simpler lifestyle. Instead of going through the regular cafeteria line at meals, they could go through a line with foods that were nutritionally balanced, but very simple. Or they could go one step further. Students could choose to be "homeless," sleeping under cardboard shelters with their sleeping bags and begging for food. They could learn firsthand what it is like to live without not only luxuries, but without some necessities as well.

What would you be willing to live without for a week?

How could elementary students participate in this Week of Prayer? In their one-room school, students range from six to fourteen years of age. Choosing to be "homeless" was not an option because younger students needed regular meals.

"I've got it!" one student finally shouted! "We can bring lunches to school each day that are totally homemade—no packages of chips, no junk food. We could bring sandwiches, no fast foods."

"What do the rest of you think?" the teacher asked the class.

"We like the idea," most agreed.

"This will be optional; no one has to participate. But if you do, write down your thoughts and feelings as the week progresses."

As twelve o'clock came around that Monday morning, there were mixed

CHOOSING GOD

reactions when students opened their lunches. "It's just the same as always. I guess my mom doesn't ever send much junk food," one student remarked. But others moaned about the lack of chips and sweets. "There isn't one package of anything!" "I have a sandwich, carrots, and an apple. No cookies!"

After three days of the lunch-time experiment, one student commented, "I'm getting used to this. And I think I've noticed something. We get along better when we eat healthier food!"

"I think we like each other more," another student joined in. "Maybe we should do this more often!"

A simple elementary-school experiment—or was it? When Jesus created people, what did He intend for them to eat? How were they to nourish this human machine that had been created in the image of God? The human body was made to operate optimally on simple, nutritious food. So how did things change so drastically? How did we become a nation of fast-food lovers?

Admittedly, we do live in a fast-paced world where often people do not take the time to prepare or to eat the healthiest meals. But maybe food is not the only issue here. A fast-paced world means that people are in a hurry. What happens to rest, exercise, and devotional time in that type of environment? God created us as beings who function most optimally in a clean environment filled with fresh air and sunlight. Spending time outside relaxes and refreshes our minds and our bodies.

Body and mind are so closely related that whatever affects our bodies also affects our minds. Likewise, whatever affects our minds also affects our bodies. Learning to preserve our health is one of life's most important lessons. God has blessed us with an abundance of information about how to live healthy lives. He speaks to us through the Holy Spirit. "Don't copy the behavior and customs of this world, but let God transform you into a new person by changing the way you think. Then you will learn to know God's will for you, which is good and pleasing and perfect" (Romans 12:2). Our physical habits affect our bodies. God will show us what changes to make when we listen to His voice.

In this sinful world, no one has perfect health, a perfect mind, or a perfect body. Nothing is an absolute guarantee against disease, but following a healthful diet, getting plenty of rest and exercise, and spending time with God do make a definite difference. Any positive changes make a difference. But how do we make changes that are lasting, changes that become habit?

The human brain is amazing. As acts are performed again and again, the pathways, or neurons, become more efficient, stronger. Remember when you first learned to tie your shoes? It took a lot of concentration and several tries. But now you don't even think about the action. You may be talking to someone and not aware of the messages going from your brain to nerves and muscles in order to accomplish the task. Reaching for healthful food rather than empty-calorie treats can eventually become an automatic choice. Reaching for your Bible as you begin and close your day can become your habit. Going to bed in time to get adequate rest can become part of your lifestyle.

What would you say to someone who says how they take care of their body is their own business?

We have talked about foods, nutrition, rest, exercise, fresh air, sunlight, and spending time with God. What are the other components to make the healthiest lifestyle? Our bodies need water. We use water to wash our hands and our clothing. Water is also a necessity in helping our bodies be cleansed from impurities. Our brains operate better so we can think more clearly when we drink at least eight glasses of water each day. One student reminded his classmates to bring their water bottles by making a computer graphic entitled "Brain-wash, anyone?" This play-on-words emphasizes the importance of keeping our brains and bodies hydrated with fresh water.

God knows what our bodies need to work efficiently. He knows what we need to be able to think clearly. Because Satan is keenly aware that if we follow all the principles we have talked about in this lesson, we will be drawn closer to our Maker, he works to present temptations that draw us away. Harmful substances such as alcohol, tobacco, and drugs not only bring adverse effects to our bodies, they affect our thinking, thus inhibiting our ability to make good decisions. The safest pathway to choose is to always stay away from these damaging substances.

You might ask, what about the person who has already made some poor decisions? We were created by a God of love, a God of forgiveness. In His wisdom and grace, He will gently lead us to make changes that improve our bodies and empower us to become more like Him both in body and in mind.

CHOOSING GOD

Journal

- What habits do you have that contribute to a healthy body? A healthy mind? What habits do you think you should change?

Dig a Little Deeper

1. One of Jesus' miracles of healing is recorded in Matthew 9:1–8. Read that story and the following passage and answer the following questions:

   "The paralytic found in Christ healing for both the soul and the body. The spiritual healing was followed by physical restoration. . . . There are today thousands . . . who, like the paralytic, are longing for the message. 'Thy sins are forgiven.' . . .They can find no relief until they come to the Healer of the soul. The peace which He alone can give would impart vigor to the mind, and health to the body" (*The Desire of Ages*, p. 270).

   a. In what way was the man's physical health changed?
   b. In what way was the man's spiritual health changed?
   c. In what way do you think his mental health was changed?

2. Read Matthew 9:1–8; Psalms 41:4; 103:1–3; and Jeremiah 3:22. What categories of healing are mentioned in the Bible texts? Explain why you believe God is willing to heal in each of these areas.

3. Discover some of the changes that will take place in your life as you grow into Christ's likeness.

   a. How will you grow mentally? 2 Timothy 2:15
   b. How will you grow spiritually? Matthew 22:39; Proverbs 16:32; Galatians 5:22, 23; John 14:15
   c. How will you grow physically? 1 Corinthians 6:20; 10:31; Colossians 3:23

4. The eight remedies listed in the lesson introduction not only have physical benefits but also can be thought of as symbols of spiritual benefits. List each remedy and suggest a spiritual benefit for each.

Activities

A. Plan two physical-fitness activities to use with the younger children in your school. Give information to students telling how these activities benefit the body.

B. God's plan for good health is often different from the general thinking in society. Gather articles and advertisements for diets, over-the-counter medications, etc. Compare and contrast these with the eight principles of health. Tell if the articles and ads are addressing the symptoms or the cause. Select a health-related topic to research. Choose a method to share your findings with the class.

C. Make a pie chart of the way you spend your time each day. Make another pie chart showing improvements you could make to better meet the laws of health taught in the eight natural remedies.

D. When God made time, He made enough of it (Celtic saying). Explain this statement. How does it apply to our society?

To Learn More

Counsels on Diet and Foods
Counsels on Health
The Ministry of Healing
Vibrant Life

CHOOSING GOD

"See how much our Father loves us, for he calls us his children, and that is what we are! But the people who belong to this world don't recognize that we are God's children because they don't know him" (1 John 3:1).

No matter what we have done or who we are, we are of infinite worth to Jesus, our Creator and Savior. He illustrated our worth when He said, "What is the price of two sparrows—one copper coin? But not a single sparrow can fall to the ground without your Father knowing it. And the very hairs on your head are all numbered. So don't be afraid; you are more valuable to God than a whole flock of sparrows" (Matthew 10:29–31). If we are so valuable, why is it that sometimes we just don't feel good about who we are?

You Are Special to Him

Psalm 51

David listened to the story Nathan, the prophet, was telling him. His heart went out to the poor man who had his pet lamb taken from him. He was incensed that anyone could be so thoughtless, so uncaring, so . . . Then Nathan hit David with the truth, and David realized the magnitude of his own crimes and the chasm that separated his actions from his values, his ideals. David realized that his sins separated him from what God wanted him to be. He wrote his reaction in Psalm 51:

Have mercy on me, O God,
    because of your unfailing love.
Because of your great compassion,
    blot out the stain of my sins.
Wash me clean from my guilt.
    Purify me from my sin.
For I recognize my rebellion;
    it haunts me day and night.
Against you, and you alone, have I sinned;
    I have done what is evil in your sight. . . .
Purify me from my sins, and I will be clean;
    wash me, and I will be whiter than snow.
Oh, give me back my joy again;
    you have broken me—
    now let me rejoice.
Don't keep looking at my sins.
    Remove the stain of my guilt.
Create in me a clean heart, O God.
    Renew a loyal spirit within me

        (verses 1–4; 7–10).

CHOOSING GOD

The psalmist's feelings of degradation come through as he asks God for a new heart, for forgiveness. One can understand his pleas for forgiveness based on his actions and the enormity of his sins. When we do something wrong, those feelings of sin, separation, and guilt can lead us to seek forgiveness. The Holy Spirit continues to speak to us until we come to God for restoration.

When have you experienced the Holy Spirit speaking to you?

Sometimes we might feel bad, not because of something we have done, but because of who we are, or aren't. We may feel bad because of what we don't have, or because of who others say we are. How can these feelings happen when one is committed to Christ? Why does so much seem wrong when one is following Jesus? These questions are not unique to any individual. Everyone has feelings of inadequacy at times. Sometimes it helps to know that others experience the same feelings. At other times, that is no comfort.

The question remains: If we are children of God and are choosing to follow Him, why do we still sometimes feel worthless? The answer may be quite complex, but it also can be simple. Here are some possibilities:

- We live in a sinful world. Satan tries every avenue available to him to convince us that we are not worthy to be accepted by God.
- Almost everyone feels at times that he or she doesn't measure up to others. Everyone has a bad day or difficult times. Some people hide their negative feelings better than others are able to.
- In a world of sin where emphasis can be on possessions, on externals, it is sometimes easy for one to place self-worth on objects, power, or position.
- Everyone has a unique personality. What bothers one person may not impact another.

Sometimes when looking at others, we make the assumption that the inside, the way the other person feels, is just as polished and in control as the outside appearance. However, with most individuals, there is some degree of feelings of inadequacy and doubt.

During her academy years, a young girl moved to a new school. Even though she made friends, she didn't feel accepted and struggled to fit in. At times she felt awkward. When it came time for her ten-year academy reunion, she debated whether or not she wanted to attend. Did she once again want to deal with the feelings she had experienced in academy? She decided to go and was very surprised to learn that many students expressed that they had felt the same way during their school experience. She realized that the ones who had picked on her are just people. Classmates she thought were popular and secure had insecurities too. Everyone struggles at times to fit in. It is an emotion common to human beings.

Had the girl changed or had her perspective changed?

Perhaps another question should be asked. What creates a person's value? The media wants us to believe that the value lies in what one purchases or looks like. We are bombarded in advertising with the idea that one can be better with a certain product or purchase. But that is not where the answer is found. Instead, the answer lies in the fact that we are created in God's image: "God said, 'Let us make human beings in our image, to be like ourselves'" (Genesis 1:26). Because God created us to be like Him, our worth must lie in that fact. He created us, He loves us, He died for us. We are of value because of who God is and the value He places on us.

Do you realize how valuable you are to God?

By continually spending time with God, allowing the mind to dwell on His character and focus on His plans, humans who may be so consumed by the moment, can have a broader focus. In this way, we can gain perspective that keeps the important parts of life in the forefront and places the rest where they belong.

We read stories of individuals who turned their feelings of inferiority or failure into great service for others. This outward focus on creating or helping can make a difference. For example:

- Thomas Edison once said that he did not see his experiments as failures. Instead, he discovered over one thousand ways not to create a light bulb. But he persisted and succeeded.
- Albert Einstein didn't do well in school, but his brilliant mind and great discoveries inspire us today.
- Marie Curie, a great scientist whose work with radium still influences cancer treatment, said, "Nothing in life is to be feared. It is only to be understood."

CHOOSING GOD

- Abraham Lincoln, known as one of the greatest United States presidents, failed his first attempt to be elected to Congress and failed when he ran for the Senate.
- Eleanor Roosevelt was known for her grace, sensitivity, and understanding, despite a childhood that lacked love and recognition.

Think for a moment of Bible characters you have studied who saw their worth because of their position in Christ. In Luke 1:38, Mary, the mother of Jesus, called herself the "Lord's servant." She saw her worth not in her situation, but rather because of who God is. Amos testified to his inadequacy for the job of a prophet. "'I'm not a professional prophet, and I was never trained to be one. I'm just a shepherd, and I take care of sycamore-fig trees. But the LORD called me away from my flock and told me, "Go and prophesy to my people in Israel"'" (Amos 7:14, 15).

Mary wasn't chosen because of her influence on the town of Nazareth. She was chosen because she knew who God was. Amos wasn't chosen because of his desire to be a prophet. He was chosen because he knew who God was. God knew He could trust Mary to bear His Son. He knew He could trust Amos to carry His messages to Israel. Sometimes when we feel the least qualified, we are the most dependent upon God. That is often when God can use us to work for Him. He is always there. We can trust Him. We can trust His love. We can trust His promises. Feelings of insecurity will no doubt arise at times. No matter what we experience, we can be confident of God's love. "I will never fail you. I will never abandon you" (Hebrews 13:5). Because of God, we are of infinite value.

CHOOSING GOD

Journal

- What would you like to say to God in response to this lesson?

Dig a Little Deeper

1. Answer the questions below.
   a. To whom do we belong? Read 1 Corinthians 6:19, 20
   b. What clue can you find in Galatians 1:4 that gives you an idea of how valuable you are to God?
   c. Romans 5:8 and John 3:16 tell us something about the kinds of people God says are of great value to Him. Who does He say are included?

2. Name at least two Bible characters who felt they were not worth much until Jesus helped them realize their worth. Tell how Jesus treated them and how this changed their lives. Give references for your findings.

3. In talking to people about how valuable they are to Him, Jesus used illustrations of two very ordinary things. What are they? What do you think He meant? Luke 12:6, 7

4. We can begin to understand how much we are worth to God not only by what He does for us now, but also by what He has planned for us in the future. What are these plans? 1 John 2:25; 1 Corinthians 2:9

5. Think about a plan for your life.
   a. What qualities do you value in yourself? In others?
   b. What strong points in yourself could you reinforce?
   c. What faults or problems would you like to change?
   d. Select a Bible text that could be your mission statement or statement of commitment.

6. Psalm 8 gives a God's-eye view of His children and the value He places on them. After reading it, answer the following questions.
   a. How does this psalm make you feel about God?
   b. How does it make you feel about yourself?
   c. What do you think the psalm says about the way God feels about people?
   d. What do you think the psalm means when it says that God crowned people "with glory and honor"?

Activities

A. Write a short prayer, a poem, an acrostic, or a slogan expressing thankfulness for who you are.

B. Using a concordance, research Bible verses that testify to the fact that we are children of God. Choose one and share your passage with the class and discuss how it shows you are incredibly precious to Him. Make a card of your favorite passage and give it to a shut-in.

C. Write a "Guess Who" quiz about students in your room. Do not use the persons' looks as clues. Choose specific and positive characteristics. Here are some sample questions. Guess who:
   1. wants to be a computer programmer when he grows up?
   2. always has a good idea for a good game?
   3. is helpful to the younger children?
   With your teacher's permission, give the quiz to your classmates. (Negative clues should not be written.)

D. Bring pictures of yourself to class and make a "Who's Who in Our Classroom" bulletin board. Under each picture put a favorite Bible text of that person.

To Learn More

Amos 1; 2; 7
Luke 1
Patriarchs and Prophets, chap. 71

Jesus established His church to carry on the work He started, to encourage those who believe in Him, and to spread the gospel to those who do not know Him. Examine what it means to be a Seventh-day Adventist Christian as you become like Him.

unit 5

UNDERSTANDING GOD

A Write the memory verses for the unit and add them to your file.

B Research recent or ongoing mission activities of the church. Locate and mark on a map at least five countries where mission activities are happening or have happened recently. Identify, if possible, the name/names of the missionaries serving in these areas.

C Invite a newly baptized Christian to your classroom to share his or her conversion experience.

D As a culminating activity for the unit, publish a newspaper covering the topics that were studied. Your paper could include feature articles about each of the lessons, artwork, an advice column, letters to the editor, photos, an editorial, or poetry.

© DARREL TANK

UNDERSTANDING GOD

Memory Verse

" 'Go and make disciples of all the nations, baptizing them in the name of the Father and the Son and the Holy Spirit. Teach these new disciples to obey all the commands I have given you. And be sure of this: I am with you always, even to the end of the age' " (Matthew 28:19, 20).

Sculpture of the first Adventist missionaries, J. N. Andrews and his children, on the campus of Andrews University

God can use everyone to help announce the Second-Advent message. Years ago in Sweden, only ministers of the state church were permitted to preach. When the Advent message reached Sweden in the early 1840s, the state clergy refused to preach Christ's second coming. Children and youth, some of whom had not yet learned to read, told of the prophecies concerning the return of Jesus. When grown men attempted to do this, they were thrown into prison, but the children could speak because they were too young to be prosecuted by the law.

In Holland, the keeper of the Royal Museum, H. Heintzpeter, was shown in a dream that Christ's second advent was near. He published his views in a pamphlet a number of years before he heard that there were Advent believers in America.

Tell It to the World

Acts 11:19–26; Revelation 14:6–10

In ancient times, Antioch was the largest and most important city in the land of Syria. It was a beautiful place where many men and women lived. People from other nations often traveled to Antioch to buy or sell and to enjoy its pleasures and luxuries.

Paul and Barnabas went to Antioch, too, but for a different reason. They had wonderful news and were eager to share it with everyone who would listen. They lived in Antioch a year, telling people about Jesus, how He had lived, and what He had taught. They described the way Jesus treated people, even those who made fun of Him and persecuted Him. They told the experiences of Jesus' illegal trial and His death for our sins. They told the amazing story of Christ's resurrection and return to heaven. They repeated the promise He had given them about the future:

> "Don't let your hearts be troubled. Trust in God, and trust also in me. There is more than enough room in my Father's home. If this were not so, would I have told you that I am going to prepare a place for you? When everything is ready, I will come and get you, so that you will always be with me where I am" (John 14:1–3).

What do you think was important to Paul and Barnabas?

Paul and Barnabas spoke with such sincerity and confidence that they had a powerful influence on those who heard them. Many people became Christ's followers. Before long those who believed in Christ were given a name that had not been used before. They talked so much about Christ that they were called Christians. That name was used in ridicule by some, but it became a

UNDERSTANDING GOD

title that Christ's followers carried proudly. Gradually the use of the name *Christian* spread. Even today Christ's followers are still called Christians.

Early in the nineteenth century, groups of Christians began to study the prophecies in the books of Daniel and Revelation. Among them was William Miller. As a result of his studies, he found the Savior the world needed. He began preaching of Christ's second coming, emphasizing the need to be ready. Many of Miller's followers felt they could determine an exact date based on the 2,300-day prophecy that ended in 1844. They determined that the actual date would fall on the Day of Atonement which, calculated from the Jewish calendar, fell on October 22.

Those who believed in the soon coming, or advent, of Christ worked diligently to tell others and to be ready themselves. When Christ did not come in 1844, they were terribly disappointed. Many of these people no longer believed that Christ would soon return. Others went back to their Bibles, studying and praying that God would help them find their error. God answered their prayers by leading them to a better understanding of the prophecy. They had been right in believing that a special event had happened on that date—it was, however, a special event in heaven. By studying and restudying the book of Daniel, they discovered that the prophet had been given a vision of a magnificent court scene in heaven.

? **How do you think you would have reacted to the terrible disappointment of 1844?**

" 'I watched,' " Daniel wrote, " 'as thrones were put in place and the Ancient One sat down to judge. His clothing was as white as snow, his hair like purest wool. He sat on a fiery throne with wheels of blazing fire, and a river of fire was pouring out, flowing from his presence. Millions of angels ministered to him; many millions stood to attend him. Then the court began its session, and the books were opened.

" 'I continued to watch because I could hear the little horn's boastful speech. I kept watching until the fourth beast was killed and its body was destroyed by fire. The other three beasts had their authority taken from them, but they were allowed to live a while longer.

" 'As my vision continued that night, I saw someone like a son of man coming with the clouds of heaven. He approached the Ancient One and was led into his presence' " (Daniel 7:9–13).

These Bible students discovered the meanings of other biblical truths. They heard from Seventh Day Baptists that God had set the seventh day apart as holy time. They studied the Bible to confirm this, found it to be true, and began to observe it. Although there have always been people who have kept the true Sabbath, to these new believers it was an exciting discovery. When they needed a name by which they could be identified, they chose to call themselves Seventh-day Adventists. They chose "Seventh-day" because they believed in and observed the seventh day as Sabbath, and "Adventist," because they believed in the advent, or second coming, of Jesus.

Early Seventh-day Adventists soon realized that people who want to keep God's commandments need to be able to think clearly so that they can understand God's instructions. They began to emphasize the importance of a healthy mind and body.

Seventh-day Adventists' understanding of Jesus' commission to His disciples (Matthew 28:19, 20) led them to begin their missionary work. The first Adventist missionary family, Elder J. N. Andrews and his young children, Mary and Charles, sailed across the Atlantic to Europe in 1874. They settled in Switzerland. Before long Elder Andrews began holding meetings and giving Bible studies. Soon he set up a small print shop and, with the help of his children, began to print and distribute numerous papers and small books explaining the beliefs of Seventh-day Adventists.

With the guidance of the Holy Spirit, Seventh-day Adventists discovered the beliefs held by the church today. One of God's chosen messengers, Ellen White, was among the early Seventh-day Adventists. She was able to give them encouragement, instruction, warnings, and hope.

Seventh-day Adventists teach many of the same beliefs taught by a number of other churches and denominations. For example, almost all Christians believe in the Trinity, or Godhead. Most believe Jesus came to this earth to save sinners and that He will come again. Almost all believe in the Bible as the inspired source of knowledge about God. Fewer denominations share our beliefs about baptism by immersion, what happens to people when they die, and the seventh-day Sabbath. Seventh-day Adventists are unique in the beliefs about Christ's ministry in the sanctuary, the court scene in heaven, and the messages of the three angels of Revelation.

What beliefs of Seventh-day Adventists are different from those of other Christians?

The great teachings of the Bible upon which the Seventh-day Adventist

UNDERSTANDING GOD

Church bases its distinctive beliefs form the center of the special message God has asked His followers to tell to the world to prepare people for the second coming of Jesus. These beliefs contain the messages that will allow all those who are willing to believe what He says, to accept what He offers, and to do what He wishes, to have a relationship with God for the rest of eternity. The only people who cannot be saved are those who reject Him. They would not be comfortable in God's perfect, sin-free universe.

"In a special sense Seventh-day Adventists have been set in the world as watchmen and light bearers. To them has been entrusted the last warning for a perishing world. On them is shining wonderful light from the word of God. They have been given a work of the most solemn import—the proclamation of the first, second, and third angels' messages. There is no other work of so great importance. They are to allow nothing else to absorb their attention" (*Testimonies*, vol. 9, p. 19).

Adventists take seriously the commission Jesus gave His disciples just before He returned to His Father: "The Good News about the Kingdom will be preached throughout the whole world, so that all nations will hear it; and then the end will come" (Matthew 24:14). This is why Seventh-day Adventists study the Bible thoughtfully, honor the seventh day of each week as God's holy day, practice generous giving of their money and time for the work of the church, and look forward to Jesus' return. They share this good news of salvation with everyone. Seventh-day Adventists believe the whole world needs to hear it. Their goal is to live in such a Christlike way that everything they say and do will help to show the whole world what God is like. What better way could be found to reveal God's character than to treat people as Jesus did?

UNDERSTANDING GOD

Journal

- Write about a time when you shared your beliefs with a friend. Were you nervous? Did you feel comfortable? Why or why not?
  OR
- Write about a time when you did not share your beliefs with a friend when you had the opportunity. How did you feel later?

Dig a Little Deeper

1. Many Christians believe that the Ten Commandments were meant only for people who lived in Old Testament times. Why do Seventh-day Adventists believe these commandments are still important today? 1 John 2:3–6; Matthew 5:17, 18

2. For most of earth's history, God's people have been in the minority. God has never promised His people the comfort of going along with the crowd. What did Jesus say about this in Matthew 7:14?

3. Perhaps you think, "I don't understand much about what my church teaches, so I don't want to make any claims I can't explain to others." What do David and Timothy have to tell you about this? Psalm 119:9–11, 130; 2 Timothy 2:15

4. Although you study the Bible, you may be afraid you will forget what you have learned if you try to explain it to others. What promise has Jesus given for people who feel this way? Matthew 10:19, 20

5. You might be concerned about people who call themselves Seventh-day Adventists, but don't seem to be very good Christians. How does Jesus say we should feel about these people? Matthew 5:43–47; 7:1–5

Activities

A. There are many stories of young people who were pioneers in the development of the Seventh-day Adventist Church. Select one of the following names or another of your choice. Become that person and present your story to the class or for chapel.

> William Farnsworth
> Rachel Oakes Preston
> John N. Loughborough
> Uriah Smith
> J. N. Andrews

> Annie R. Smith
> Mary Andrews
> Ellen White
> James White
> John Harvey Kellogg

B. Check with your local conference communication and/or education department for audio-visual materials relating to the church's mission outreach program or find information on www.adventistmission.org. Write a mission story to share with the lower grades.

C. The mission of the church is to share the good news with everyone. As a class, choose a way to be a missionary in your community. Possible suggestions: Collect food for your local food bank, prepare a program to present to senior citizens, make cards to send to someone who is not well or is recently bereaved.

D. As a class, read aloud the messages of the three angels in Revelation 14:6–11. Discuss the meaning of these messages and their importance in the Seventh-day Adventist Church.

To Learn More

The Bible Story, vol. 10, pp. 65–67

The Bible Pageant (1986), vol. 5, pp. 67, 68

Arthur W. Spalding, *Origin and History of Seventh-day Adventists* (Review and Herald® Publishing Association, 1961), vol. 1, chap. 7, "Banners of Truth"

Morris L. Venden, *The Pillars* (Pacific Press® Publishing Association, 1982)

Charles E. Bradford, *Sabbath Roots: The African Connection* (Ministerial Association of the General Conference of Seventh-day Adventists, 1999)

UNDERSTANDING GOD

Memory Verse

"As for us, we can't help but thank God for you, dear brothers and sisters loved by the Lord. We are always thankful that God chose you to be among the first to experience salvation—a salvation that came through the Spirit who makes you holy and through your belief in the truth" (2 Thessalonians 2:13).

"If something is very important in our lives, we say it is 'fundamental.' Our families are fundamental. Food is fundamental. The air we breathe is definitely fundamental!

"As Seventh-day Adventists we also believe there are spiritual things that are fundamental to our lives. Together we have made a list of twenty-eight of these beliefs, all of them based on what the Bible teaches.

"Thankfully these twenty-eight beliefs are not something we have to memorize for an exam. They are not like a math problem or a spelling quiz. They are more like an instruction manual that helps us operate our car or computer. These twenty-eight beliefs help us remember what is important in operating our lives."

Jan Paulsen, President
General Conference of Seventh-day Adventists

Seventh-day Adventists Believe

Genesis 1– Revelation 22

Our major beliefs explain how Seventh-day Adventists perceive God. They express what we believe the Bible says about His love, kindness, mercy, grace, justice, righteousness, and peace. Every belief reveals the love of God, and when properly understood, these beliefs center on Him—the Way, the Truth, and the Life.[1]

As you better understand God, your love for Him deepens, your love for others deepens, and you learn to "love the Lord your God with all your heart . . . and your neighbor as yourself" (Matthew 22:37–39).

The twenty-eight fundamental beliefs of the Seventh-day Adventist Church can be grouped into six major categories:

> God
>
> Man
>
> Salvation
>
> The Church
>
> Christian Life
>
> Last Things

The beliefs, as written in this lesson, have been summarized for the General Conference Children's Ministries Department.[2] As you read through them, pray that the Holy Spirit will help you see and remember how much God loves you.

Beliefs About God

1. The Word of God

I believe that God inspired every writer whose words appear in the Bible. Everything they wrote is true, and what they said can help me live a happy and healthy life.

UNDERSTANDING GOD

2. The Godhead

I believe that the God who loves me is actually Three Gods in One—the Father, the Son, and the Holy Spirit. Each works hard to teach me how to live a better, more meaningful life.

3. God the Father

I believe that God the Father is the Power that keeps me—and every other creature in the universe—alive. His is kind and forgiving, and will never leave me alone.

4. God the Son

I believe that God the Son, Jesus, created this world and everything good in it. Two thousand years ago, He came to this earth as a baby, grew up and lived a sinless life, then died on the cross so that I could someday live forever with Him in heaven.

5. God the Holy Spirit

I believe that God the Holy Spirit is that still, small Voice I hear in my thoughts whenever I feel afraid, sad, or lonely. It tells me that everything will be all right. The Holy Spirit also tries to teach me right from wrong by making me feel guilty when I sin and joyful each time I choose to obey God's laws of love.

Beliefs About Man

6. Creation

I believe that Jesus created everything in six days and then rested on the seventh day. When He had finished making the trees, animals, oceans, mountains, and Adam and Eve, Jesus looked around at all that He had done and said joyfully, "This is very good!"

7. The Nature of Man

I believe that Jesus made people in the image of God. All enjoy the freedom to think and act any way they want. Even though sin and bad choices have brought pain and suffering to many, we're still children of God. With the help of the Holy Spirit, we can care for each other just like God cares for each one of us.

Beliefs About Salvation

8. The Great Controversy

I believe that Satan is a real being who wants to destroy us all. He works hard each day to bring destructive sin into our lives. God wants us to live each day with joy, happiness, and love. God and Satan are fighting for control over our lives and our futures. To help us overcome sin, Jesus sends the Holy Spirit and loving angels to guide and protect us.

9. Life, Death, and Resurrection of Jesus

I believe that Jesus lived a perfect life in order to show us that it's possible to overcome sin. He died on the cross so I won't have to lose my heavenly home because of my sins. Then, God raised Jesus from the dead to demonstrate how He'll someday raise me from the dead if I die before Jesus returns.

10. The Experience of Salvation

I believe that when I allow Jesus into my heart, He helps me change from a sinner to a child of God, ready to live forever in heaven. He teaches me how to be like Him as I read my Bible and follow the loving guidance of the Holy Spirit. Thanks to Jesus, I can be confident that I'm forgiven and that there's a home waiting for me in heaven.

11. Growing in Jesus

I believe that when people invite Jesus into their hearts, changes start to happen fast. What they read, watch on television or on the Internet, eat and listen to; the places they go; even the words they say will change. The pages of the Bible will become like a textbook for living, and many whispered prayers will come from their lips. These changes keep happening, day after day, until Jesus comes.

UNDERSTANDING GOD

Beliefs About the Church

12. The Church

I believe that my church is a place where people who love Jesus can praise Him together without fear or embarrassment. It's like attending a fun family reunion each week. Jesus loves His church and listens to every word spoken and every song sung.

13. The Remnant and Its Mission

I believe that before Jesus comes the second time, some people in my church will choose sin over salvation. Those who stay faithful to the Bible and keep listening to the sweet voice of the Holy Spirit are called the remnant, and they will work extra hard to bring the love of God to the world. Though the remnant may be small in number, they'll accomplish great things for God so that Jesus can return.

14. Unity in the Body of Christ

I believe that any church whose members worship God should welcome people from any nation, who speak any language, and whose skin is any color. We're all equal in God's sight. How we look and how we sound makes no difference. We're all children of the same heavenly Father.

15. Baptism

I believe that when I'm baptized, I'm telling everyone that I love God and want to live my life in service to Him. Baptism is like being buried as a dirty sinner and then rising up to live a new, clean life for Jesus.

16. The Lord's Supper

I believe that when Jesus ate His last meal with His disciples right before He was crucified, He taught us something wonderful. He said that the grape juice (wine) represented His spilled blood and that the bread represented His broken body. When I eat "The Lord's Supper" at church, it helps me remember the sacrifice Jesus made for me on the cross.

17. Spiritual Gifts and Ministries

I believe that God has given me (and you) special talents that we can use to serve Him. We each enjoy different skills like music, preaching, teaching, art, giving Bible studies, visiting the sick, or making people feel welcome when they visit our church. Each spiritual gift is important to the work of God.

18. The Gift of Prophecy

I believe that people in God's church need help knowing how to live and what to look forward to in the future. So, God invited a woman named Ellen G. White to be His prophet and provide guidance, instruction, and correction for His people. She also helps us understand the important lessons found in the Bible. When I read what God's prophet wrote a long time ago, I'm discovering important things that God wants to say to me today.

Beliefs About the Christian Life

19. The Law of God

I believe that God's Ten Commandments contain the best rules for living. Each is designed to protect me from sin and help me stay out of trouble. Each represents how much God loves me and how He wants me to live a happy, healthy life. Obeying the Ten Commandments is like saying "I Love You" to God.

20. The Sabbath

I believe that God created the seventh day (Saturday) to be a holy day. He commands me to do special work for Him on that day as a way of showing Him—and others—that I believe He is the Creator of all good things. God's holy Sabbath begins at sundown on Friday and ends at sundown on Saturday.

21. Stewardship

I believe that everything belongs to God, the trees, the flowers, the animals—even me. God has asked me to take care of what He created and to protect all things from harm—even me. So, I will cherish God's creatures and creation. To show Him how proud I am to be His steward, I'll faithfully return a tithe, give offerings, share time and talents, and use resources responsibly. I want God to bless this world and everything in it—even me.

22. Christian Behavior

I believe that anyone who loves Jesus should talk, act, eat, work, and play differently from those who love Satan. Everything I do should show others that Jesus lives in my heart and that I'm doing my best to live by His rules of love.

23. Marriage and the Family

I believe that in order for us to understand the joy of living in heaven, God invites us to create families here on this earth. When we love our brothers and sisters, uncles and aunts, parents and grandparents, we're experiencing a beautiful example of what it will be like to live in heaven with everyone who has chosen to love and obey God. Our heavenly Father wants our earthly homes to be safe places to learn about His love and forgiveness.

Beliefs About Last Things

24. Jesus' Ministry in the Heavenly Sanctuary

I believe that God instructed Moses and the children of Israel to build a temple in the wilderness to explain what Jesus is doing right now in heaven. In the wilderness, the priests oversaw the forgiveness of sins and the judgment of those who chose to do evil. That's what Jesus is doing right now in heaven. He is our heavenly Priest waiting to forgive us, clean sin from our hearts, and finally welcome us home to heaven.

25. The Second Coming of Jesus

I believe that, one day soon, Jesus is going to return to this earth and invite everyone who has chosen to love and obey Him to heaven. When He comes, those who hate Him will be destroyed. But everyone else, even the faithful who have died in the past, will leave this dark world and spend eternity with Jesus.

26. Death and Resurrection

I believe that Jesus can raise people from the dead. He did it before (like Lazarus and the widow's son), and He will do it again when He returns the second time. So, even though some of my family sleep in the ground, I'll see them again because of the power of God over death.

27. The Millennium and the End of Sin

I believe that, someday, sin and sinners will be gone forever. My Bible says that even those who died hating God will fully understand the lies that Satan told them and will agree that God's judgment is just. Without God's presence to shield them from harm, Satan and every sinner will face the world alone and be completely destroyed by fire.

28. The New Earth

I believe that when Satan and sinners are gone, my heavenly Father will create a brand-new world for us to enjoy. There will be no death, no tears, no pain, no suffering. All will be peace and love. Best of all, I, my family, and all who love God will enjoy this wonderful world forever and ever.[2]

God is at the center of each of the twenty-eight fundamental beliefs. His greatest desire is for you to see a clear picture of His character. When you see Him clearly, you will find His love irresistible.

[1] *Seventh-day Adventists Believe: A Biblical Exposition of Fundamental Doctrines.* Pacific Press® Publishing Association. 2005.

[2] "God Loves Me 28 Ways Beliefs," by Charles Mills. In *God Loves Me 28 Ways,* by Charles Mills and Linda Koh. Pacific Press® Publishing Association. 2006.

UNDERSTANDING GOD

Journal

• What are your thoughts about the beliefs you just read? How do they show you God's love?

Dig a Little Deeper

1. Write each of the fundamental beliefs in your own words.

2. Find at least one Bible text that supports each fundamental belief.

3. How do beliefs impact behavior?

4. Do you agree with the fundamental beliefs? Explain.

5. Which of the fundamental beliefs encourage you to love God? Which beliefs encourage you to love others? Explain.

Activities

A. Create illustrations for each of the twenty-eight fundamental beliefs.

B. Create a brochure or PowerPoint® presentation that can be used to share the twenty-eight fundamental beliefs with family or friends. Use some of the illustrations created for Activity A in the brochure or PowerPoint® presentation.

C. Design activities or a game that will explain the twenty-eight fundamental beliefs to younger students in your school.

D. Create a Fundamental Beliefs Wheel. See TRM, p. 63.

To Learn More

Charles Mills and Linda Koh, *God Loves Me 28 Ways: A Kid's-eye View of the Fundamental Doctrines of the Seventh-day Adventist Church* (Pacific Press® Publishing Association, 2006)

Seth J. Pierce, *Seventh-day Adventists Believe for Teens* (Pacific Press® Publishing Association, 2007)

Memory Verse

"Jesus said to them, 'The Sabbath was made to meet the needs of people, and not people to meet the requirements of the Sabbath. So the Son of Man is Lord, even over the Sabbath!'" (Mark 2:27, 28).

It was the middle of a Friday afternoon, at the close of a desperately difficult week. Two men were sitting at a table, wearily studying charts and intricate diagrams for building a medical center. One man was a Seventh-day Adventist Christian. The other, a devoted member of another church, leaned back in his chair, sighed, and said, "You know, I don't think I could give up the freedom of my Saturdays to keep your Sabbath."

What would you say if one of your friends made this statement?

A Time to Rejoice

Exodus 20:8–11

The Sabbath is a time to remember that God is the Creator.

From the moment Adam first saw Eve, he felt she would be a perfect companion for all time. She, too, felt the joy of existence.

As that final day of Creation came to a close, God appeared to them in the Garden, and they recognized their Creator in this brilliant Being. Together they welcomed in the first earthly Sabbath. In awe they listened as He told them about the past six days, about the beginnings of all things they could see, feel, hear, touch, and taste. He had spoken the words of creation, and each day the earth had become more beautiful. Now it was theirs to enjoy.

That evening the first Sabbath began, and as the sun disappeared from view, the light of God's presence surrounded them. Adam and Eve knelt at His feet in worship. In complete joy they communed with God in the Garden and learned about the Sabbath. All work was set aside. All thoughts turned to remembering their Creator God. All praise and adoration flowed from their hearts in love.

The Sabbath was more than a thing or place. It was a time God promised to set apart to meet with the ones He loved. This day was given to them for their happiness. It was a special time for God to meet with the crowning act of His creation—to get to know each other heart to heart.

What was the purpose of Sabbath in the Garden of Eden?

Adam and Eve must have listened in amazement as God told them about their world and the beings on other worlds He had created. They must have felt blessed as the first Sabbath came to an end and God invited them to spend every Sabbath with Him.

UNDERSTANDING GOD

The Sabbath is a time to remember that God offers freedom.

We do not know how long Adam and Eve lived in the Garden of Eden or how many Sabbaths they enjoyed face-to-face friendship with Him. We do know that after Adam and Eve left the Garden, the Sabbath was still a special day of worship.

Many years later, God said to the children of Israel, " 'Be careful to keep my Sabbath day, for the Sabbath is a sign of the covenant between me and you from generation to generation. It is given so you may know that I am the LORD, who makes you holy' " (Exodus 31:13).

During the centuries they were in Egypt, God's people forgot the Sabbath. They were slaves so long they had almost forgotten God. When they escaped from Egypt, they did not know God well enough to trust Him.

One way God could teach the people to trust Him was by providing for their physical needs. They traveled in safety. No one became sick. No one was thirsty or hungry. And God taught them lessons as He gave them water, shelter, and food.

Daily, people went out and gathered manna, the food God sent from heaven. They gathered enough for only one day. None could be saved for the next day, for it would spoil.

On the sixth day of each week, however, the people needed to gather twice as much manna and save half of it for the Sabbath. On Sabbath there was no manna to gather. Moses warned them:

> " 'This is what the LORD commanded: Tomorrow will be a day of complete rest, a holy Sabbath day set apart for the LORD. So bake or boil as much as you want today, and set aside what is left for tomorrow.'
>
> "So they put some aside until morning, just as Moses had commanded. And in the morning the leftover food was wholesome and good, without maggots or odor. Moses said, 'Eat this food today, for today is a Sabbath day dedicated to the LORD. There will be no food on the ground today. You may gather the food for six days, but the seventh day is the Sabbath. There will be no food on the ground that day' " (Exodus 16:23–26).

Week after week the double portion of manna God sent on the sixth day reminded the people that the seventh day was the Sabbath. " 'Remember,' "

Moses said, "'that you were once slaves in Egypt, but the LORD your God brought you out with his strong hand and powerful arm. That is why the LORD your God has commanded you to rest on the Sabbath day'" (Deuteronomy 5:15). God did not command them to keep the Sabbath in order to limit their freedom. The command was given to remind them that He was the One who had set them free—free from Egyptian bondage and free to worship Him in peace and safety.

God did not give the Sabbath just to the people of Israel. He gave it to all people everywhere. His offer of freedom is for anyone who chooses to accept it.

The Sabbath is a day to remember that the One who created us has the power to re-create us into His likeness.

When Jesus lived on earth, He said, "'The Sabbath was made to meet the needs of people'" (Mark 2:27). Jesus reminded them that He was Lord of the Sabbath. He had created the Sabbath and demonstrated during His life how it should be kept.

What two things does the Sabbath remind us that Jesus did for us?

It was Jesus' custom to go to the synagogue on Sabbath to worship. Many times He taught from the prophecies explaining His mission. One Sabbath as He was teaching, He healed a man's deformed hand. When criticized, Jesus answered, "'The law permits a person to do good on the Sabbath'" (Matthew 12:12). During another Sabbath service, Jesus healed a crippled woman. He was delighted to free her from Satan's bondage. Imagine how the man who had been ill for thirty-eight years felt that Sabbath when Jesus cured him. He certainly understood the Scripture that says the Sabbath is to be a time of delight!

After His crucifixion, Jesus rested in the tomb through the hours of the Sabbath. But nothing could keep Him there, for the One who died on the cross for our sins is also the all-powerful Creator of the universe. In the early morning after the Sabbath, Jesus arose from the dead and came out of the grave. On that bright morning, while the sorrowing disciples were mourning the loss of their Lord, the universe was celebrating the victory He had won at the cross.

Christ, the One who came to save us, is also the One who created us.

UNDERSTANDING GOD

When we keep the Sabbath, we are demonstrating our faith that Jesus is our Creator, our Savior, and our God. The same Creator who rested that first Sabbath in the Garden of Eden rested in the grave. The first time, He rested from the work of creation. The second time, He rested from His work of redemption or *re*-creation. Since Christ's resurrection, we have another reason for remembering the Sabbath. Jesus offers us eternal salvation through the blood He shed on the cross.

For all eternity, each Sabbath will be a time of celebration and joy.

By observing the Sabbath, we show that we are looking forward to the day when God will welcome His earthly family to heaven. Imagine that first Sabbath in heaven. Picture God inviting you to join in the celebration. You look around in amazement at a gathering so immense that no one can count all those who are there: the Father, the Son, the Holy Spirit, angels, beings from all the universe—and you!

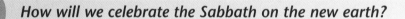

How will we celebrate the Sabbath on the new earth?

From one Sabbath to another, God's people will gather to worship Him (Isaiah 66:23). They will express their happiness and gratitude, their faith, and their love for a wonderful God. Each Sabbath will be a special time of happiness and fellowship.

UNDERSTANDING GOD

Journal

- Write about a time when you experienced a special Sabbath. What and/or who made it special?

Dig a Little Deeper

1. How much time did God measure off for each day of Creation week? For each Sabbath? Genesis 1:5, 8, 13, 19, 23, 31; 2:1

2. Many Bible authors wrote about the importance of the Sabbath. Genesis 2:1–3; Exodus 20:8–11; 31:15–17; Isaiah 58:13, 14; Ezekiel 20:20. Use your own words to explain:
   a. Why God gave us the Sabbath.
   b. Which day of the week is the Sabbath.
   c. How God asks us to observe the Sabbath.
   d. What He tells us to avoid doing on the Sabbath.
   e. What keeping the Sabbath shows about our friendship with God.

3. God gives us examples of how Jesus spent the Sabbath.
   a. Describe two things Jesus did on the Sabbath day. Luke 13:10–13; 14:1–4.
   b. Describe three things you do or could do to make the Sabbath a day of joy.

4. The Israelites in the prophet Amos's day had many rules about what they should do and should not do to observe the Sabbath. They obeyed these rules carefully because they thought they had to in order to win God's favor. But they did not enjoy the Sabbath. They were much more interested in their business than in getting acquainted with God. He described their attitude: "You can't wait for the Sabbath day to be over" (Amos 8:5). Write in your own words what God told Amos to say to them. Amos 5:21–23.

5. We can prepare all week long to keep the Sabbath holy in our homes and in our hearts. What can you do during the week to prepare for the Sabbath?

6. Some people believe that the Sabbath is for Old Testament times only and that we do not need to keep it today. Many believe that when Jesus died, He did away with the Sabbath or changed the day of worship to Sunday. What evidence do we have that the Sabbath was kept after the Resurrection? Acts 13:14, 15; 17:1–3; 18:4.

Activities

A. Choose one of the miracles Jesus performed on the Sabbath. Write it as a dialogue. Practice it with a group of your classmates to present for worship at school or at Sabbath School.

B. The Sabbath is sometimes called "the world's birthday." Create something to illustrate the greeting "Happy Birthday, World!" You may choose to create a poster, a wall hanging, a birthday card, or a poem.

C. Planning ahead helps to make the Sabbath a time of happiness. Following are some suggestions for projects that can add joy to your Sabbath. Plan to complete one or more.
    1. Locate people in your community who have special knowledge about nature. Arrange for a Sabbath afternoon nature walk led by a nature specialist.
    2. Jesus performed many of His healing miracles on the Sabbath in order to show that caring for the needs of the lonely and ill is proper on His holy day. Plan to visit some people in your community who are sick or lonely.
    3. Ask a leader to help you arrange for a group to meet on Sabbath afternoon to sing, share, or study the Bible.

D. Go to www.puzzlemaker.com. Create one of the puzzles using key words from this week's lesson. Print the puzzle and the key. Make copies of your puzzle to share with the class.

To Learn More

The Bible Pageant (1986), vol. 4, pp. 73–78
The Bible Story, vol. 1, pp. 57–60; vol. 2, pp. 143–145;
    vol. 8, pp. 75–78; vol. 9, p. 138

UNDERSTANDING GOD

"We died and were buried with Christ by baptism. And just as Christ was raised from the dead by the glorious power of the Father, now we also may live new lives" (Romans 6:4).

When Jesus commissioned the disciples to preach the gospel to all nations, He also told them to baptize those who believed. Through the centuries, Christians have considered baptism a special ceremony necessary to the Christian life. Seventh-day Adventist Christians believe that baptism by immersion as demonstrated by Jesus best symbolizes the significance of the ceremony.

A New Life in Christ

Matthew 3:13–17

Rumors floated around Jerusalem. Something was happening out in the desert beyond the Jordan River. A young preacher named John was proclaiming, "Repent of your sins and turn to God, for the Kingdom of Heaven is near" (Matthew 3:2). Long before, the prophet Isaiah said this would happen someday (Isaiah 40:3). Now this man announced that the Messiah was coming—soon!

John spoke boldly about the corruption in the nation and fearlessly pointed out the sins of the people who came to hear him. His words were so plain and clear that many were convinced that what he was saying was true. The people, however, thought the Messiah would come as a king and make them the greatest nation on earth. They wanted to be sure they would be ready to welcome Him. "What shall we do?" they asked anxiously. When John explained they should repent and be baptized, many of them did.

One day as John was preaching, a young Man edged His way through the crowd. There was something different about this Man. As John watched Him approach, the Holy Spirit told John that he was looking at the Messiah. When the young Man asked to be baptized, John hesitated. " 'I am the one who needs to be baptized by you, . . . so why are you coming to me?' " (Matthew 3:14).

How did John know it was the Holy Spirit speaking to him?

"But Jesus said, 'It should be done, for we must carry out all that God requires' " (Matthew 3:15). John baptized Jesus, not because He was in need of cleansing, for Jesus had never sinned. He was baptized to set an example for us. "After his baptism, as Jesus came out of the water, the heavens were opened and he saw the Spirit of God descending like a dove and settling on him. And a voice from heaven said, 'This is my dearly loved Son, who brings me great joy' " (Matthew 3:16, 17).

Jesus' baptism, in addition to being an example for us, signified:

- The moment of decision—the time to begin the work for which He had come.
- The moment of identification—the time when the Father and the Holy Spirit gave visible and audible proof of their relationship with Him.
- The moment of approval—God's voice speaking to Jesus, "This is my dearly loved Son."
- The moment of acknowledgment—the symbol of a dove showing continual presence with Jesus, strengthening Him for His work.

Ever since that day, the ceremony of baptism has had great meaning for Christ's followers. Baptism signifies that the Holy Spirit has led the sinner to confess his wrongs, to accept God's forgiveness, and to acknowledge Jesus as his Lord and Savior. "At our baptism we pledged ourselves to break all connection with Satan and his agencies, and to put heart and mind and soul into the work of extending the kingdom of God" (Ellen G. White Comments, *SDA Bible Commentary,* vol. 6, p. 1075). The apostle Paul compared baptism to dying and then being raised to a new way of life: "We died and were buried with Christ by baptism. And just as Christ was raised from the dead by the glorious power of the Father, now we also may live new lives" (Romans 6:4).

Baptism is a statement and ceremony of commitment. It is the beginning of a grown-up journey in which fellow Christians pledge support and invest in the new member's spirituality. To progress on this journey, it is important to remember that:

- Growing in faith takes daily commitment. "My righteous ones will live by faith" (Hebrews 10:38). God promises to continue making changes in you as you strengthen your relationship with Him. "I will take out your stony, stubborn heart and give you a tender, responsive heart. And I will put my Spirit in you so that you will follow my decrees and be careful to obey my regulations" (Ezekiel 36:26, 27).

- Cleansing comes from confessing sins each day. "If we confess our sins to him, he is faithful and just to forgive us our sins and to cleanse us from all wickedness" (1 John 1:9). Repentance and recommitment are ongoing. By continually coming to God, you renew your strength. "Go back to what you heard and believed at first; hold to it firmly. Repent and turn to me again" (Revelation 3:3).

- Turning away from temptations is possible when you turn to Jesus for strength. "The temptations in your life are no different from what others experience. And God is faithful. He will not allow the temptation to be more than you can stand. When you are tempted, he will show you a way out so that you can endure" (1 Corinthians 10:13). You still will be tempted. In fact, temptations may be stronger, for the evil one recognizes your commitment to Jesus and will be deliberate in drawing you to sin. Paul describes this conundrum in his life in Romans 7:19. "I want to do what is right, but I can't. I want to do what is good, but I don't. I don't want to do what is wrong, but I do it anyway." He claims the victory in verses 24 and 25 of the same chapter. "Who will free me from this life that is dominated by sin and death? Thank God! The answer is in Jesus Christ our Lord."

You have made your choice to follow Jesus, and the Holy Spirit is only a prayer away. This new beginning, which started with baptism, is a sign of promise to live a life committed to God. You have become a member of God's family of faith.

UNDERSTANDING GOD

Journal

- Have you made a decision to be baptized? Why or why not?

Dig a Little Deeper

1. According to the Bible, what should happen before a person is baptized?
   a. Acts 2:38, 41
   b. Acts 16:30, 31

2. Read the following texts and describe how a person is to be baptized.
   a. Acts 8:36–39
   b. Matthew 3:13–17
   c. Colossians 2:12
   d. John 3:23
   e. Mark 1:5

3. Baptism is a public statement to others that something has happened in one's life.
   a. What is symbolized by going under the water? Romans 6:3, 4
   b. What is symbolized by coming up from the water? Romans 6:5
   c. How will a life be different because of baptism? 2 Corinthians 5:17

4. Reread the narrative to discover at least three things that baptism signifies or represents. Write a paragraph to summarize what you learned.

Activities

A. Write a story that would describe the conversations that took place in the meeting of the Ethiopian and Philip or of Christ and Nicodemus. See Acts 8:26–38 and John 3:1–21.

B. Use a concordance to find names of people who were baptized. Choose one and make a diorama or mural about the event. The scriptural index and the general index in the back of *The Desire of Ages* and *The Acts of the Apostles* will assist you in locating information.

C. Interview a member of your church who has been baptized. Where were they baptized? When? How old were they? Who baptized them? Who attended their baptism? How did they feel? Write a report to share their story with your class.

D. Research the beliefs of other churches to discover different baptismal rites that may be conducted. At what age are people baptized? Who participates in the ceremony? Who conducts the service? When and where is it done? Use a graphic organizer to present your findings.

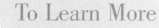

To Learn More

The Bible Story, vol. 7, pp. 93–108
The Bible Pageant (1986), vol. 4, pp. 42, 43
The Desire of Ages, chap. 11
Messiah, chap. 11

Memory Verse

"Every time you eat of this bread and drink of this cup, you are announcing the Lord's death until he comes again" (1 Corinthians 11:26).

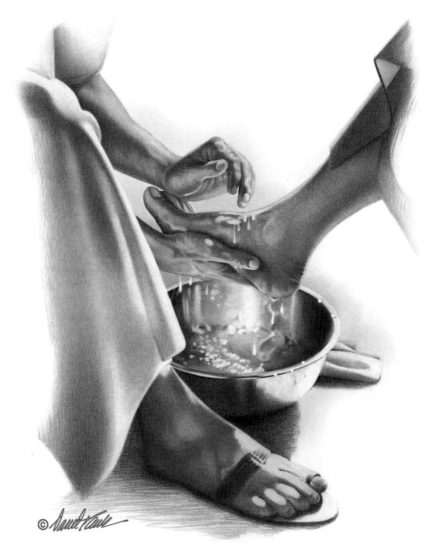

© David Hale

The way Seventh-day Adventists observe the Lord's Supper, or Communion, is based on the actual events that took place between Christ and His disciples on Thursday evening just before He was crucified. The first part of this ceremony, the footwashing, is a dedication, similar to baptism.

In the second part of the Lord's Supper, the bread and grape juice are symbols that point both to the past and to the future. This ceremony looks back to Jesus' death on the cross as our Redeemer, and ahead to when He will redeem His people from the effects of sin. How does the Bible describe that event? How did Jesus explain its meaning?

In Remembrance of Me

John 13:1–20; Matthew 26:26–30

On a Thursday in early spring, families all over Jerusalem had gathered in their homes to celebrate the Passover. It was a time to remember the night, more than a thousand years before, when God had rescued their ancestors from slavery in Egypt. Year after year the story had been handed down from parent to child. In each family the parents told the story that their parents and grandparents had told to them.

On the tenth day of the first month of the year, each family was to choose a lamb or a young goat for a sacrifice. The animal was to be a perfect one-year-old male sheep or goat. On the fourteenth day of the month, the animal was to be slaughtered at sundown. Some of the blood of the slaughtered animal was to be put on the doorposts and above the doors of the homes where the animal would be eaten. That night the meat was to be roasted and eaten with bitter herbs and bread made without yeast. The people were to eat it quickly and be prepared to leave immediately after the meal as their ancestors had done years before.

The Passover was meant to be a time for happiness, but in the room where Jesus and His disciples had gathered to observe it, there was jealousy and suspicion. The twelve men who were Jesus' dearest friends had been squabbling about which one of them was the greatest.

More than three years had passed since Jesus and John had met at the Jordon River, where Jesus had begun to gather His group of followers around Him. Now, Jesus' mission on earth was almost complete. There were still many things He wanted to help His disciples understand. If only they had been ready to listen! Instead, they eyed each other resentfully. Each one wanted the highest place in the kingdom they thought Jesus was about to establish. Each disciple thought that his loyalty and his talents were not appreciated as they should be.

UNDERSTANDING GOD

Do we quarrel about these kinds of things?

In those days it was the custom for a servant to wash the feet of the guests. A pitcher of water, a basin, and a towel were ready, but no servant appeared. Each disciple knew that he should take the servant's place, but each one was too proud to do so. Instead, they all pretended not to notice the pitcher and basin.

The room was quiet. Jesus got up from the table and picked up the towel and basin of water. He did not condemn His friends for quarreling among themselves. Instead, the Creator of the universe knelt down before His disciples and washed their feet! Imagine how those men felt as one by one they looked down on Jesus' head and bent back, watching as He washed the dust from their feet and dried them with a towel.

The men were humiliated. As Jesus moved from one to another, they began to realize that while they were so concerned about being great, Jesus was concerned about serving them. As the dust was washed away, their feelings of jealousy and pride gradually changed to feelings of sorrow for the way they had acted. The Passover meal that began with quarreling and bitterness became a time of repentance, forgiveness, and new beginnings for all of them except Judas.

While Jesus was washing Judas's feet, the disciple had a sudden desire to admit he had agreed to betray Jesus. But he was too proud. He could not bring himself to confess his sin and ask to be forgiven. He decided that if Jesus could lower Himself to do the work of a servant, He certainly could never be Israel's king. The more Judas thought about it, the more certain he became that there was nothing for him to gain by continuing to follow Christ. He made up his mind to proceed with his plan to betray Jesus.

What effect did Jesus' act of washing Judas's feet have on his final decision to betray the Master?

After Jesus had finished washing His disciples' feet, He sat down and began to talk to them as they ate the Passover meal.

"Do you understand what I was doing?" He asked them. "You call me 'Teacher' and 'Lord,' and you are right, because that's what I am. And since I, your Lord and Teacher, have washed your feet, you ought to wash each other's feet. I have given you an example to follow. Do as I have done to you. I tell you the truth; slaves are not greater than their master. Nor is the messenger more important than the one who sends the message. Now that you know these things, God will bless you for doing them" (John 13:12–17).

At the Passover supper, Jesus began a new celebration, now called the Communion service. "Jesus took some bread and blessed it. Then he broke it in pieces and gave it to his disciples, saying, 'Take this and eat it, for this is my body.' And he took a cup of wine and gave thanks to God for it. He gave it to them and said, 'Each of you drink from it, for this is my blood. . . . It is poured out as a sacrifice to forgive the sins of many'" (Matthew 26:26–28). Imagine the disciples' stunned silence and confusion. *Jesus' body? Given for them? His blood? To be poured out for them? What could He mean?* They listened in bewilderment. "'Do this to remember me as often as you drink it. For every time you eat this bread and drink this cup, you are announcing the Lord's death until he comes again'" (1 Corinthians 11:25, 26). The disciples heard what Jesus said, but they did not understand He was speaking of the sacrifice He would soon be making.

Days later, after Jesus' death and resurrection, they remembered His words, and at last they began to understand His command to "remember Me."

Remember His love for all His earthly family.

Remember His humble service for others.

Remember His willingness to forgive.

Remember His death and resurrection.

Remember His power to heal and restore His whole creation, to "make all things new."

Ever since that evening, the ceremony of washing one another's feet has been a reminder that God is always willing to cleanse His children from sin if they will confess. The Passover was a reminder of the Israelite slaves' deliverance from Egypt. The Communion service is a reminder of deliverance from the power of sin and guilt. It is a reminder that the One who created everything in the universe gave it all up to become a man who "humbled himself in obedience to God and died a criminal's death on a cross" (Philippians 2:8).

The Communion service is designed to keep the hope of Jesus' second coming alive in our minds. Each time you celebrate this sacred service, think about the symbols and their meanings. While you are washing someone's feet, let your mind wander to the Creator of the universe bending to wash the dusty feet of His disciples. Allow the Holy Spirit to impress upon you the privilege of humbly serving others. As you eat the bread and drink the grape juice, the symbols of Christ's body and blood, consider Jesus' sacrifice in dying for our sins so we may have eternal life. Think . . . remember . . . and share in memory of Him.

UNDERSTANDING GOD

Journal

- How did you feel the first time you participated in a Communion service? OR
- Give your thoughts and feelings about the Communion service.

Dig a Little Deeper

1. Imagine that a friend of yours who is not a Seventh-day Adventist comes to church with you on the day when you are celebrating the Communion service. Your friend has never seen this kind of religious ceremony before and is very curious. After the service your friend asks you to explain what each part of the ceremony means. What would be a good explanation of the meaning of (a) footwashing, (b) the bread, and (c) the wine?

2. Use the story of the Last Supper in John 13:12–17 to answer the following questions:
   a. What question did Jesus ask His disciples?
   b. What instructions did Jesus give the disciples?
   c. To whom does Jesus liken a person who washes another's feet?
   d. Why do you think Jesus used the example of a slave?

3. There are various ways of celebrating the Lord's Supper, but most Seventh-day Adventist churches follow the same practices. It's usually celebrated four times yearly.
   a. Should it be celebrated more often? Less often? Why?
   b. Does a person have to be a baptized member of the Seventh-day Adventist Church before taking part in the Lord's Supper? (See the *SDA Church Manual.*)
   c. What church officers are involved in the preparation for the Communion service, in the service itself, and in the clean up? What is the responsibility of each?

4. Why do Adventists use bread made without yeast and unfermented fruit juice in the celebration of the Lord's Supper?

5. It is a common practice to read from 1 Corinthians 11:23–26 during Communion service.
   a. Who wrote these words? (Look for a clue at the beginning of the book of 1 Corinthians.)
   b. Where did he get the information in these verses?
   c. On what night was the Lord's Supper first eaten?
   d. What do Christians announce when they eat the Lord's Supper?

Activities

A. Discover some of the Passover customs and symbols used in Jewish celebrations of the Passover today. Tell what these customs and symbols mean.

B. With your pastor, plan and participate in a Communion service with your class. If possible, invite other church leaders such as elders, deacons, and deaconesses to assist.

C. Prepare and deliver a report on unleavened bread. Include ideas such as where it originated, what it represents, how it is prepared, how it is used today. Find a recipe or see TRM, page 88, prepare, and share with the class.

D. How did the Israelites celebrate the Passover that last night before they left Egypt? (Exodus 12:1–11). How did they celebrate it after they reached the Promised Land of Canaan? (*The Desire of Ages*, pp. 76, 77, 273–279, 653). What is the difference between the two Passover celebrations and why? Chart your findings on a Venn diagram.

To Learn More

The Bible Pageant (1986), vol. 4, pp. 140–143
The Bible Story, vol. 9, pp. 55–64
The Desire of Ages, chap. 72
Messiah, chap. 72

Memory Verse

"The Lord himself will come down from heaven with a commanding shout, with the voice of the archangel, and with the trumpet call of God. First, the Christians who have died will rise from their graves. Then, together with them, we who are still alive and remain on the earth will be caught up in the clouds to meet the Lord in the air. Then we will be with the Lord forever. So encourage each other with these words" (1 Thessalonians 4:16–18).

Throughout history there have always been both a curiosity about death and a fear of it. To the Christian, death is not a mystery. The Bible tells us very plainly that death is like a sleep and that we will rise when Jesus comes to earth again.

When Death Comes to the Christian

Ecclesiastes 9:5

Do you know what I am?" asked the lady who sat before us, attached by tubes to a continuous flow of oxygen. Before we could respond, she continued, "I am a witness! I can't do much anymore," Ruth explained to her visitors, "but one thing I can do is be a witness!" Though in her nineties, she still had the same sparkling eyes and smile. "Every night I am so tired. I pray that the Lord will just let me sleep. Just let me sleep until Jesus comes. But each morning when I wake up, I thank Him for not answering my prayer. He has given me one more day to witness for Him. I write letters. I send books to people. I encourage them because I am a witness. As long as the Lord is willing to let me witness for Him, I will keep on telling people how wonderful He is."

Ruth knows what to expect when she finally does die. She knows with confidence that she will sleep until Jesus comes again to take His children home to live with Him forever. Hearing Jesus call her from the grave is something to which she looks forward. The future isn't mysterious to Ruth.

Why do you think God makes what happens after death so plain to us?

Death does not come only to people who live for many decades. It comes to people of all ages. Ruth has lived a full, long life. Not everyone does. What happens when death strikes the young child, the tiny infant, the full-of-life teenager, the loving parent? In these instances, death can be so unexpected. The pain of sorrow, loneliness, hurt, and loss can feel overwhelming. Knowing what happens after death doesn't mean that Christians don't grieve. Death is always a time of sorrow. It is recorded that Jesus wept at Lazarus's tomb (John 11:35). Healing takes time. But for those who have learned to trust God, there is a hope, a certainty, a peace. It is the same hope that Jesus gave to Martha and Mary the day He stood with them beside the tomb where they had placed their brother, Lazarus. It is the same certainty that Stephen expressed when he faced those who were stoning him (Acts 7). It is the same peace that Paul conveyed in Philippians 1:21, 22 when he showed confidence whether he faced life or death.

Jesus, who woke Lazarus from the sleep of death, says, "'I am the resurrection, and the life. Anyone who believes in me will live, even after dying'" (John 11:25). The One who conquered death will someday wake all who died believing in Him. The Creator will re-create each of His faithful children at the resurrection. He knows them all. He remembers everything about them. Their private memories, their personalities, their characters are all preserved in the Creator's mind.

No one looks forward to suffering or death, but Christians know that there is something beyond these experiences. They can face eternity with hope and with joy that is founded on confidence in God. Like Paul, they can say, "I know the one in whom I trust, and I am sure that he is able to guard what I have entrusted to him until the day of his return" (2 Timothy 1:12).

What a day that will be! Try to imagine Christ calling: "'Awake, awake, awake, ye that sleep in the dust, and arise!' Throughout the length and breath of the earth the dead shall hear that voice, and they that hear shall live. . . . From the prison house of death they come, clothed with immortal glory. . . . And the living righteous and the risen saints unite their voices in a long, glad shout of victory. . . .

"Little children are borne by holy angels to their mothers' arms. Friends long separated by death are united, nevermore to part, and with songs of gladness ascend together to the City of God" (*The Great Controversy*, pp. 644, 645).

What do you think of when you read this description of the resurrection?

UNDERSTANDING GOD

Journal

- What would you say to or do for someone who has just lost a loved one?

Dig a Little Deeper

1. The question about what happens when a person dies is one that has challenged people's thoughts for thousands of years. To find out what the Bible has to say about the meaning of death, notice God's formula for creating a human being. You will find this formula in Genesis 2:7. It tells what parts He put together and what special title He gave to the finished product.

   _____ + _____ = _____

2. Find words or phrases that describe what happens to a person when he dies. Job 34:15; Psalms 104:29; 146:4; Ecclesiastes 9:5; 12:7

3. Death is not the end of existence for people who trust God. After reading 1 Corinthians 15:53 and John 5:25, copy and complete the following sentence: I believe that death is not the end of existence because of the promise that . . .

4. Describe what happens to the living righteous and the resurrected righteous at the Second Coming. 1 Corinthians 15:51–54; 1 Thessalonians 4:16, 17

5. Read Ellen White's description of what will happen when Christ comes. Complete the sentences below:
   "Christ came to restore that which had been lost. He will change our vile [sinful] bodies and fashion [make] them like unto His glorious body. . . . All blemishes and deformities are left in the grave. Restored to the tree of life in the long-lost Eden, the redeemed will 'grow up' (Malachi 4:2) to the full stature of the race in its primeval [original] glory. The last lingering traces of the curse of sin will be removed, and Christ's faithful ones will appear in 'the beauty of the Lord our God,' in mind and soul and body reflecting the perfect image of their Lord" (*The Great Controversy*, p. 645).
   a. Thinking about this great event makes me . . .
   b. What I have read in this lesson helps me understand that for a Christian, death is . . .

Activities

A. Compare and contrast news and entertainment (newspapers, TV, books, and movies) views of life after death with the Bible references you studied in Dig a Little Deeper.

B. Most people need help in coping with death. That is a time when Christians who know God can offer comfort and hope. We need to think of ways to help those who are grieving. Here are some suggestions:
- Listen to the person talk about how he or she feels. Do not interrupt.
- Stay with the person for companionship. Sometimes it is hard to be around someone who is grieving. You may want to get away, but think first of how the person feels. You may not know what to say to your friend. What you say is not important. Just being there is.
- Offer some practical help. Run errands, do dishes, take clothes to the cleaners. Do whatever you can to make it easier for your friend.
- Continue to be a friend even though your friend may not be much fun for a while. Your friendship is especially needed now.

Write practical suggestions of something you could do to help in the following scenarios:
- Your best friend's father dies. What can you do to help your friend?
- After a long illness, your neighbor's wife dies. They have two children, a seven-year-old boy and a two-year-old girl. What can you do to help this family?
- A classmate is killed in a car accident. What can you do for the family?
- Has someone close to you died?
  - What were your reactions to this death?
  - How did others help you?
  - How did you help others?

C. Use objects and/or processes in nature to illustrate death and resurrection. Your illustrations could be words or pictures. Ideas might include cocoon and butterfly; falling leaves, barren trees, spring growth; bulbs and flowers.

D. Invite someone from a local hospice or a support ministry such as Stephen's ministry, to talk with your class about the services they provide.

To Learn More

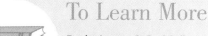

Ecclesiastes 9:5; 12:7

Laura Rocke Winn, *Margie Asks, Why do People Have to Die?* (Review and Herald® Publishing Association, 1999)

27

UNDERSTANDING GOD

" 'Bring all the tithes into the storehouse so there will be enough food in my Temple. If you do,' says the LORD of Heaven's Armies, 'I will open the windows of heaven for you. I will pour out a blessing so great you won't have enough room to take it in! Try it! Put me to the test!' " (Malachi 3:10).

" 'I will open the windows of heaven for you. I will pour out a blessing so great you won't have enough room to take it in! Try it! Put me to the test!' " (Malachi 3:10). This is a promise from God. Seventh-day Adventists and other Christians have been quietly proving this miraculous promise for many years. The promise is available to anyone who sincerely follows the instruction God has given. What are the windows of heaven?

Windows of Heaven

Malachi 3:7–12

I n the beginning, God . . ." God created, God provided, God gave. Today God still creates, provides, and gives. He creates each of us as individuals with unique talents. He provides us with daily blessings. He gives lavishly to us. Think of the last present you received. Where did it come from? A parent? A friend? But where did it come from before they gave it to you? Perhaps it came from a store in the mall or from a warehouse in another parish, province, or state. Keep tracing the path your present took before it reached you. Did it come from another country? As you continue, where do you think the search will eventually end? Finally it will be traced to resources from our earth, resources created by God.

All of the talents, time, and resources we possess come from God. They are gifts that He entrusts to us. Because God gives, or blesses, so generously, He asks that we be responsible in the way we use these gifts. In working to develop skills and talents, we learn to be more like Jesus. He told about this in Matthew 24:45–47, where He describes the faithful servant. When the master returned and found that the servant had done a good job, he rewarded him. In Matthew 25:14–28, Jesus tells a similar story in which He compares the kingdom of heaven to a man going on a trip. Before leaving, he gave one servant five bags of silver, one servant two bags of silver, and one servant one bag of silver. Upon the man's return, the servant who was given five bags brought him five more. In the same way, the servant given two bags earned two more. To each of these two the master responded, " 'Well done, my good and faithful servant. You have been faithful in handling this small amount, so now I will give you many more responsibilities. Let's celebrate together!' " (Matthew 25:21, 23). But the third servant, the one who buried his talent in the ground, was told he was wicked and lazy.

These bags of silver given to the servants represent more than just money.

They represent any of the talents, abilities, resources, and time that God gives. When we value what He has given, we learn to set priorities. We realize the importance of all resources, making sure there is time in the day to practice, to help, to conserve, and to share.

What resources can you think of that are available to you?

All day long we are using resources. The amount of paper, energy, and chemicals used has an effect on our world and on others living on the earth. The adage "Let us live simply so others can simply live" is a reminder to be good stewards so others can have what they need.

God gave precise advice in dealing with some blessings. We read of Melchizedek accepting tithe from Abram and of the Israelites paying tithe, or returning one-tenth of their increase to God. Why should God ask people to return tithes and give offerings to Him? He says that all the silver and the gold of the world, all the animals of the field and forest, the cattle on thousands of hills are His. He does not ask for tithes and offerings because He needs them. His greatest interest is not in money but in hearts and minds and motives. Giving offerings is one way of teaching us to think about the needs of others. Concern for others can help us learn to use what God gives wisely and unselfishly. Giving reminds us that everything comes from Him. When we give God our gifts cheerfully and with grateful appreciation, even the smallest amount is priceless. Such giving is really an act of worship.

What is more important to God than our money?

Jesus talked with the Pharisees about giving. He said, "You are careful to tithe even the tiniest income from your herb gardens, but you ignore justice and the love of God. You should tithe, yes, but do not neglect the more important things" (Luke 11:42). Tithing is important and necessary, but there is something more important.

When we learn to use our talents, time, money, and other resources responsibly, others are blessed. The Bascoms, owners of a truck and auto company in the Midwest, are glad to find opportunities to help others using what God has given them. "Because of God's blessings to us, we have been fortunate to have been able to help many others with their needs," said Mr. Bascom. "Sometimes we have been able to do repairs for free. Sometimes we have given someone a vehicle for free. Sometimes we just help someone move or give them a ride to church."

When the Bascoms were first married, they contemplated whether or not tithing was worthwhile. They soon started to notice a difference between the weeks in which they did and did not pay tithe. On the weeks after they returned tithe, business boomed. They have advice for people who are struggling with the concept of stewardship. "You're dealing with the Creator of the universe, who owns everything. He's given us a promise that says, 'Test Me. Try Me and see if I won't give you more blessings than you're able to receive.' I think that's a pretty safe gamble, and people should try it. People aren't going to realize the benefits of tithing if they don't try."

How can it be a blessing to you when you give to others?

Jesus commented on an act of giving that has encouraged givers for two thousand years. One simple deed has inspired many to give no matter how little they have. No gift is too small. One day He and some of His disciples were in the temple court as people were dropping their gifts into the collection boxes. "A poor widow came by and dropped in two small coins. 'I tell you the truth,' Jesus said, 'this poor widow has given more than all the rest of them. They have given a tiny part of their surplus, but she, poor as she is, has given everything she has'" (Luke 21:3, 4).

Do you think people would give the same amount if no one else knew what they gave? Why or why not?

Giving, no matter what the gift, how small or large, can sometimes bring unexpected and far-reaching results. The Loma Linda University Heart Team had arrived in Vietnam to operate on children who desperately needed care. After they had arrived, they had been told that they might not be able to perform any surgeries. As they sat at a long council table, the ambassador leaned forward and said, "Dr. Coggin, I had dinner the other night with a good friend of yours." Certain that he must have her confused with someone else, Dr. Coggin just smiled. He went on to say he had dined with Queen Frederica of Greece. "She told me about your work and what a good thing you do. I had some false information, but she clarified that for me. Now we are very eager for you to get started."

Between 1967 and 1969, the heart team had made three trips to Greece.

On one of those trips, Dr. Coggin learned that the queen was a vegetarian. Upon returning home, Dr. Coggin sent the queen an assortment of vegetarian foods and cookbooks from the Loma Linda Market. During the ensuing years when the queen needed more, she would send a telegram, and Dr. Coggin would ship her several cases of vegetarian food.

Because of the good reputation established with Queen Frederica, the team was able to operate on patients in Vietnam. Children could lead healthy, normal lives as a result of a kind gesture of sharing. The advice in Proverbs 18:16 proved to be true. "Giving a gift can open doors; it gives access to important people!"

When we give, God blesses us. He "will open the windows of heaven." He will give to us. Then, through giving we learn to appreciate our blessings. We become aware of what we have, of what we are receiving. We no longer take these things for granted, and we begin to understand how our blessings can be used for others.

Paul wrote to the believers in Corinth, asking for offerings on behalf of the believers in Jerusalem. "Remember this—a farmer who plants only a few seeds will get a small crop. But the one who plants generously will get a generous crop. You must each decide in your heart how much to give. And don't give reluctantly or in response to pressure. 'For God loves a person who gives cheerfully.' And God will generously provide all you need. Then you will always have everything you need and plenty left over to share with others." "As a result of your ministry, they will give glory to God. For your generosity to them and to all believers will prove that you are obedient to the Good News of Christ. And they will pray for you with deep affection because of the overflowing grace God has given to you" (2 Corinthians 9:6–8, 13, 14).

Having people pray for you is a blessing. It is one of the unexpected benefits of being generous.

How could having someone pray for you be a blessing?

Perhaps, you are thinking, that all of this talk about talents, time, money, and resources seems relevant to people who are much older than you are. Perhaps this will be important when you have completed school and have a job. Remember the story Jesus told about the very small offering, and think for a moment about ways you can demonstrate and practice responsible stewardship.

- Return one-tenth of your increase to God as tithe.
- Set aside offerings in addition to your tithe.
- Develop the talents God has given you.
- Respect the resources God has given us in the earth by using them wisely and sparingly.
- Remember to spend a portion of your time learning about God, talking with Him, and helping others.

Then the King will say to you, "You have been faithful!"

UNDERSTANDING GOD

Journal

- Complete several of the following sentences:
    I have found that money is . . .
    Money can buy . . .
    One thing I will never do with my money is . . .
    One good thing about having a large amount of money is . . .
    One problem that might come from having a large amount of money is . . .
    One reason people don't give larger offerings is . . .

Dig a Little Deeper

1. Look up *stewardship* in the dictionary. Choose the definition that most appropriately fits this lesson. Explain why you chose that definition.

2. Tithe paying goes back a long, long way in history. Your Bible says that Abraham and Jacob paid tithe. Genesis 14:18–20; 28:22. Based on the information in these experiences, how much tithe should one return on an allowance of $17.50, $30, $45 per month?

3. What besides money did the Israelites bring as tithes? 2 Chronicles 31:5, 6. What words tell you that the Israelites were bringing these tithes with a glad heart?

4. When Jesus lived in Palestine, many people were following God's instruction to Moses carefully. However, Jesus condemned them for their hypocrisy. Summarize what they were doing and why it was wrong. Matthew 23:23

5. The Bible not only speaks of tithe, but it also speaks of offerings. Offerings may be for missions, church expense, Adventist education, community needs, disaster relief, and other projects. List the principles that apply to any offerings. Deuteronomy 16:17; 2 Corinthians 8:12; 9:7; Proverbs 19:17

6. When Moses called for gifts to build the sanctuary in the wilderness, how did the people respond? Summarize the people's attitudes and the results of their gifts. Exodus 35:21, 22; 36:4–7

Activities

A. God has given the rich resources of our world. We are responsible to Him for their proper use. Many organizations are working to protect our environment by establishing programs to maintain clean air and water and to preserve forests and wilderness areas. Other projects include efforts to save endangered species of plants and animals and to clean up hazardous waste sites. Select an area of our environment that concerns you. Collect information about one of these programs and prepare a report of your findings.

B. Time is our most precious possession. How we spend it gives a good indication of what we think is important. "Of no talent He [God] has given will He require a more strict account than of our time" (*Christ's Object Lessons*, p. 342). Make a pie chart to show how you spend a twenty-four-hour period. Respond to the following questions:
    1. Do I set aside a certain amount of time every day to devote to God?
    2. Do I give time to my family?
    3. Do I give time to help others?
    4. Do I use time for myself?
    5. Is there a balance between the amount of time I use for myself and what I share with others?

C. Work with your teacher to invite your pastor or a conference representative to your class to give a report on how tithes and offerings are used by the Seventh-day Adventist Church organization.

D. Research to find the salary of an occupation that may be your future employment. Based on this salary, develop a budget. Be sure to include the principles you have studied in this lesson.

To Learn More

The Bible Story, vol. 6, pp. 189–192; vol. 9, pp. 141–144
Counsels on Stewardship

As a growing Christian, you will become aware of the responsibility of belonging to the church. Becoming a mature Christian means widening your circle to encompass the needs of the world and to carry out the gospel commission as you become like Him.

unit 6

SHARING GOD

While You're Studying

A Write the memory verses for the unit and add them to your file.

B As a class, prepare a manual on how to welcome a new student to your school or classroom.

C Prepare a scrapbook of texts, poems, pictures, and quotations that give reassurances of God's love for the family and for individuals.

D As a culminating activity for the unit, publish a newspaper covering the topics that were studied. Your paper could include feature articles about each of the lessons, artwork, an advice column, letters to the editor, photos, an editorial, or poetry.

© DARREL TANK

28

SHARING GOD

"Children, obey your parents because you belong to the Lord, for this is the right thing to do. 'Honor your father and mother.' This is the first commandment with a promise: If you honor your father and mother, 'things will go well for you, and you will have a long life on the earth'" (Ephesians 6:1–3).

The family is a sacred institution created and ordained by a loving God to help us understand and learn about Him. As you read this statement, do you heartily agree, or do you think about the differences between the ideal and what one sometimes sees from day to day? What can a student do to plan now for a happy family in the future?

What Is a Family?

Deuteronomy 6:6, 7

Morgan sits quietly watching as the organ plays and the wedding participants slowly walk to the front of the church. Her mind wanders and she feels the sadness grip her as she thinks over the past few months. She had always dreamed of getting married, of having her dad walk her down the aisle to her waiting groom. But now what would happen to that dream? Who would walk her down the aisle on that distant someday? Her world had changed so quickly when her dad died unexpectedly. Not only was her future shattered; her present changed with just one telephone call.

When she crawled out of bed that morning, she was wrapped in the security that family provides, the kind of security one takes for granted. Now it is different. Mom shows her bravery and courage in so many ways, but her eyes show her sadness. She seems tired, too, now that she has gone back to work. Dreams . . . will the family ever feel whole again?

God created the family in Eden when He created earth, stars, fish, birds, animals, and the Sabbath. He walked daily in the Garden with Adam and Eve, teaching them and talking with them. Yet even with day-to-day contact with their Creator, Adam and Eve chose a course of behavior that would alter their family life forever. God then implemented an alternative plan, a redemptive plan that would instead save humanity forever.

As we study families of the Bible, we notice that some families had problems, that even though God was the center of the home, they encountered difficulties. Think for a moment about the familiar story of Joseph. The hatred and jealousy of his brothers reached to the low of deceit and cruelty when they sold him into slavery and lied to their father. But in time, the characters of those men began to change. Even though they had been "envious, turbulent, deceptive, cruel, and revengeful . . . they were shown to be unselfish, true to one another, devoted to their father" (*Patriarchs and Prophets*, p. 225).

SHARING GOD

It could not have always been pleasant for Joseph, but one day he was able to see how and why God had led him into Egypt. God's plan was possible because Joseph made a decision to choose to follow God's will.

Another biblical family that experienced tumultuous times was that of Jesus. Gentle and submissive, He tried to please those around Him. But His brothers as well as the rabbis believed that His strict obedience to the law of God was stubbornness. "His brothers felt that His influence went far to counteract theirs. He possessed a tact which none of them had, or desired to have. When they spoke harshly to poor, degraded beings, Jesus sought out these very ones and spoke to them words of encouragement" (*The Desire of Ages*, p. 87). He dealt with false accusations and the jealousy of His brothers.

"Jesus tasted all of the bitterness of life. Many cruel people pointed at Him and whispered rumors about His birth—that His mother had been pregnant before she married Joseph. If He had responded with even an impatient word or look, He would have failed to be the perfect example He was born to be" (*Messiah*, p. 58). Some people avoided Jesus because of the way His life made them look. "When His brothers called Him a coward for refusing to join them in doing something wrong, His answer was, 'God's Word says, "The fear of the Lord is wisdom; to stay away from evil is understanding"'" (*Messiah*, p. 58). Jesus lived in a family and dealt with gossip, unkindness, and jealousy just as people sometimes have to deal with in today's world.

Because families are composed of individuals, of human beings, every family has flaws. The effects of sin are seen in our world and in our families. But just as one can still see the creative power of God in nature, one can still see the love of God in families. Think about terms used to describe families: nuclear family, blended family, step-family, single-parent family, biological family, adoptive family. The list could go on. As the adjectives change, there is differentiation between the types of families. But that is not the important part. The noun *family* is the key word. It shows sameness. Sometimes a family can even be composed of a group of nonrelated individuals, a group of people who care. That is why we use the term *church family*. Jesus' disciples and His friends Mary, Martha, and Lazarus became much like a family to Him. They were His closest friends; they shared His purpose and mission. Caring, nurturing families can do much to help one understand God's love.

Just as verb tenses can be past, present, or future, the family affects our lives by what has happened in the past, what is happening now, and what we want to happen someday. While what has happened in the past may have an effect in one's present family, plans can be made to develop habits that will change the patterns in one's future family. You can plan for the future, and at the same time you can develop traits that can affect your present family. How can this be?

"You must commit yourselves wholeheartedly to these commands that I am giving you today. Repeat them again and again to your children. Talk about them when you are at home, and when you are on the road, when you are going to bed and when you are getting up" (Deuteronomy 6:6, 7). If God gave this advice to parents so they could teach His love and ways to their children, wouldn't it be beneficial to begin following it long before one becomes a parent? Could it make a difference to you, in your family now? The practical advice given below may be helpful as you live in your family.

Eight Ways to a Happier Home

1. Pray that God will give you the strength and insight to be a source of kindness, patience, love, and understanding at home.
2. Be a good listener. Try as hard to understand other family members' points of view as you would like them to try to understand yours.
3. Realize that every home has some problems.
4. Don't be harder on your parents' mistakes than you want them to be on yours. Tolerance and forgiveness can make any home a more comfortable place to be. And they are highly contagious!
5. Remember, you're not the only one who cares. Your parents want to solve or avoid problems in the family too. Tell them you want to help.
6. Don't use home problems as an excuse for doing foolish or irresponsible things. That will only complicate the problems.
7. If your family is having trouble, it is not your business to broadcast this to the world. However, there are some types of problems that must be told to a responsible adult.
8. Remember that many of God's people have grown up in homes that were far from ideal. You have a choice in the way you respond in any situation.

Throughout the Bible God provides us with examples of different aspects of living together as a family. He showed the dangers of parents who give in to children in the story of Samson. He showed the problems that arise when a parent and child do not wait for His plan in the story of Jacob and Esau. He showed the wonder of redemptive love in the story of Hosea.

SHARING GOD

God's plan is that every home should be:

- a place of safety and happiness
- a place where we can fail, fall down, get up, and try again
- a place where we can learn discipline, responsibility, fair play, as well as tenderness, kindness, and courtesy
- a place where we learn to share
- a place where the love we share helps us understand our heavenly Father's love for us
- a place in which to get ready for a home in heaven

As you grow up, you may feel that you are ready to make many of your own decisions and be more independent than your parents want you to be. Remember the story of the talents in Matthew 25? "'The master said, "Well done, my good and faithful servant. You have been faithful in handling this small amount, so now I will give you many more responsibilities. Let's celebrate together!"'" (Matthew 25:23). The same is often true within the family. As one proves to be responsible in some areas, more privileges are given. Maturity is shown as one develops the attributes of patience. When one develops the ability to communicate without becoming angry, to listen as well as talk, trust and understanding grow and develop. As that happens, parents often realize that their children are maturing and ready to handle more responsibilities.

If the process seems slow, if you still have difficulty communicating or getting along with your family, remember that you are never alone. Since Jesus endured many difficulties in His childhood and youth, He understands each feeling and every difficulty you may have as you live and grow in a family. You can trust Him. You can confide in Him. You can go to Him any time with any problem. He provides strength, comfort, guidance, and the promise that one day we will live in the family of heaven with Him.

SHARING GOD

Journal

- What do you want to decide right now about the family you will have someday?

Dig a Little Deeper

1. List at least four ways you can show your family that you are mature enough to be trusted to make some of your own decisions.

2. People often look back to the "good old days" when things were less complicated than they are today. However, since sin entered Eden, there have always been problems. Identify the following Bible families, giving a text or chapter where the story may be found:
   a. Father showed partiality to one son and gave him special clothes.
   b. Mother sent son to live with priest in temple. The priest's sons were wicked.
   c. Brother cheated his twin and deceived his father.
   d. Although they obeyed God's command not to cut son's hair, parents gave him whatever he wanted.
   e. Older brother made fun of Him because He would not do wrong.
   f. Mother had to send her son at age twelve to live in the palace.
   g. Brothers had reputation for bad temper and intolerance.
   h. One brother killed the other brother.

3. In Ephesians 4, Paul gives a number of dos and don'ts for happy family living. After reading Ephesians 4:24–32, make two columns. In one, list all the things Paul says to do. In the other, list all that Paul says to avoid.

4. Some children and young people feel rejected and think that no one cares what happens to them. The promise in Psalm 27:10–14 can be a comfort in such a situation. Summarize the text in your own words.

5. Parents are responsible for making important decisions for their children. After reading Exodus 20:12 and Ephesians 6:1–3, tell what you believe are the responsibilities of the children.

Activities

A. Cut words, phrases, and pictures from magazines to illustrate your ideas about what makes a happy Christian family. Create a collage.

B. Plan and present a Sabbath-evening worship for your family. Here are four suggestions:
   1. Prepare an object lesson using one large candle and enough smaller candles so that each person may have one. Place the large candle where all can see it and distribute the smaller ones. Light the large candle and then read John 8:12. Explain that this candle is a symbol of Jesus, the Light of the world. Read Matthew 5:14–16 and invite family members to light their candles from the large one. Explain that by doing so they are demonstrating their desire to let Christ shine through their lives. As each one lights his or her candle, you might ask him to describe something he has done to share his light with others during the week that is ending. After all the candles have been lighted, sing a hymn together and close your worship with a prayer.
   2. Have each member of the family bring a favorite Bible text to read or quote from memory. Take turns sharing these texts and explaining their meanings. (If family members might not have a favorite text, have some written on cards or marked in a Bible that they could read.)
   3. Ask some family members to present a pantomime of a Bible story without using any props, just motions and gestures. See if others can guess the story.
   4. Ask each family member to tell the nicest thing that has happened to him or her during the week. Close the worship by having each member offer a one-sentence prayer of thanksgiving for these good happenings.

C. Think of two ways you can show someone in your family that he or she is special to you. Consider choosing a grandparent, uncle, aunt, or cousin, as well as the members of your immediate family.

D. Copy and complete these sentences:
   1. One new insight I have gained from this lesson is . . .
   2. Home is . . .
   3. For me, happiness at home is . . .
   4. Three things I depend on my family for are . . .
   5. Three things my family depends on me for are . . .
   6. Three things I depend on God for are . . .

To Learn More

James 1–5
The Desire of Ages, chaps. 9; 49
Messiah, chaps. 9; 49

SHARING GOD

Memory Verse

"There are 'friends' who destroy each other, but a real friend sticks closer than a brother" (Proverbs 18:24).

Don't look now! Within a dozen feet from where you are sitting, there are probably several of the most powerful sources of happiness that you will ever find outside of your own family. Few things in life are as important as friends. What are the qualities of friendship?

What Is a Friend?

Colossians 3:12–15

Have you ever thought of what it means to be a friend? Jesus suggests a surprising answer: "'You have heard the law that says, "Love your neighbor" and hate your enemy. But I say, love your enemies! Pray for those who persecute you! In that way, you will be acting as true children of your Father in heaven. For he gives his sunlight to both the evil and the good, and he sends rain on the just and unjust alike'" (Matthew 5:43–45). It is not natural for people to treat each other in the way Jesus described. Loving an enemy, helping someone who hates us, praying for someone who treats us spitefully is really not a natural way for any of us to act. It takes God's miracle of healing to make such a change in our behavior. This change is accomplished not by might nor by power but by God's Holy Spirit in our minds.

Peter Miller and Michael Wittman lived in Ephrata, Pennsylvania, during the days of the American Revolutionary War. Peter was a Baptist pastor. Michael hated Peter and did everything he could to abuse and oppose the pastor. One day Peter discovered that Michael had been arrested as a traitor to his country and had been sentenced to die.

The pastor set out on foot to see his good friend General George Washington, who was many miles away in Philadelphia. When Pastor Miller arrived and was admitted into the general's presence, he urged General Washington to save the life of the condemned man.

"No, Peter," was the reply. "I cannot grant you the life of your friend."

"My friend!" exclaimed the pastor, "he is the bitterest enemy I have."

"What?" asked Washington in astonishment. "You have walked seventy miles to save the life of an enemy? That puts the matter in a different light. I will grant the pardon."

And Peter Miller took Michael Wittman from the very shadow of death, back to his own home in Ephrata—no longer as an enemy, but as a friend.*

Friendship, that feeling of warmth, appreciation, and kindness between people, is a two-way street. There must be giving as well as taking. Are you a giving person? Or are you a person who only takes? A taking person's attitude says, "Be my friend. Be interested in me just for my sake. Be interested in my projects, my problems, my ideas, and my personality. Notice me. Spend time with me doing the things I like to do."

A giving person, like Peter Miller, is quite different. A giving person accepts the Bible's counsel to "give, and you will receive" (Luke 6:38). This advice can apply to the gift of friendship as well as to other kinds of giving. Everyone has something to give. We all were born with the capacity to love other people. That means you can reach out with confidence to be a friend.

A giving person's attitude says, "You are important. Your projects, your problems, your ideas are important. I'd like to spend time with you and share my ideas with you. I'd like to spend time with you doing things we both enjoy." Friendship grows when you give it away.

Almost everyone has a few close or best friends. These are individuals who like what you like, who do the things you do, and who are always there when you need them. Best friends tell you the good things in their lives as well as their problems. They are friends in whom you can confide. You know they will not betray your confidence. They are there to help you, and you are ready to help them.

Becoming close friends takes time—lots of time. While you may have many friends, you will have time for only a few close friends. They must be chosen carefully. Such friends have a great influence on you, so they should be people who love God and have the values you prize. Your parents can be close friends. When you marry you will be happiest if your husband or wife is your best friend.

? *Is there a difference between being friendly and having close friends?*

Friendship includes showing unselfish, genuine interest, not only in your special friends, but also in others. It is important for you to understand that some people really need friendship. You can help them by being their friend, but do not allow them to keep you from maintaining other friendships. Sometimes people become possessive and want to occupy all your time. Explain to them that it does not mean you like them less when you are with other friends. Tell them kindly that sometimes you need to be with other people and do other things. While not permitting them to dominate all your time, try not to neglect them.

One of the problems you may have to face as a giving person is how to deal with a person you really do not like. Pray for him or her, not just once, but regularly. Tell the Lord frankly what you don't like about the person. Perhaps he irritates you or is unkind to you or makes fun of you. Talk to the person too. You might begin by saying, "I felt bad when you . . ." Then tell him specifically how what he did hurt you. Be honest about the problem. While it may not change the person for whom you are praying, it is likely to change your attitude toward him. Maybe he acts the way he does because he needs a friend. Maybe you would feel differently about him if you knew him better. Your concern for him might be just the thing that could make him a different, more likable person. Christian friendship is like that. It reaches out with respect and courage to share with others the happiness that comes from knowing Jesus as the greatest Friend of all.

How should you relate to someone you don't really like?

Another kind of problem you may have to solve as you work to develop Christian friendships is your concern about the opinion of others. If you are too concerned about what your friends think of you, or about being different from them, it may be that you do not feel very good about yourself. You may think that it is always necessary for you to do what others do or to agree with whatever they say in order to get along with them. This is not true. Real friends respect each others' feelings and convictions. When differences arise, they do their best to disagree agreeably.

The pressures to be like everyone else are tremendous. Think about pressures you are likely to experience and decide how you will respond to them before you face a problem with the group around you. You may be urged to try harmful substances or to behave in ways that you know are wrong. Don't be ashamed or afraid to say No. Most teenagers usually respect people who have the courage to live up to what they believe, even though they may tease and make fun of such people. Paul's counsel to his friends in Rome—not to copy the behavior and customs of the world, but to be new and different people inside—is still a safe guide for you to follow. If you do, you will learn from your own experience how God's ways will really satisfy you.

How can you deal with friends who pressure you to do things you don't want to do?

Of course others in the group may believe in the same things you do but feel too timid to let the rest of the group know. It takes great courage to

SHARING GOD

stand up for what one believes and to oppose the group when they are wrong. But if you have that kind of courage, you may be able to help someone else to do the same. And in the process you may even find a new friend.

The apostle Paul once wrote a letter to the members of the church at Rome. In it he had quite a bit to say about friendship. Here is a part of Paul's letter:

Dear Friends in Rome:

"Let me say first that I thank my God through Jesus Christ for all of you, because your faith in him is being talked about all over the world. God knows how often I pray for you. Day and night I bring you and your needs in prayer to God, whom I serve with all my heart by spreading the Good News about his Son."

"Don't just pretend to love others. Really love them. Hate what is wrong. Hold tightly to what is good. Love each other with genuine affection, and take delight in honoring each other. Never be lazy, but work hard and serve the Lord enthusiastically. Rejoice in our confident hope. Be patient in trouble, and keep on praying. When God's people are in need, be ready to help them. Always be eager to practice hospitality.

"Bless those who persecute you. Don't curse them; pray that God will bless them. Be happy with those who are happy, and weep with those who weep. Live in harmony with each other. Don't be too proud to enjoy the company of ordinary people. And don't think you know it all!

"Never pay back evil with more evil. Do things in such a way that everyone can see you are honorable. Do all that you can to live in peace with everyone.

"Dear friends, never take revenge. Leave that to the righteous anger of God. For the Scriptures say,

> *'I will take revenge;*
>> *I will pay them back,'*
>> *says the LORD.*
> *Instead,*
>> *'If your enemies are hungry, feed them.*
>> *If they are thirsty, give them something to drink.*
>> *In doing this, you will heap burning coals of shame on their heads.'*
> *Don't let people conquer you, but conquer evil by doing good.*

"Therefore, accept each other just as Christ has accepted you so that God will be given glory.

"I pray that God, the source of hope, will fill you completely with joy and peace because you trust in him. Then you will overflow with confident hope

through the power of the Holy Spirit" (Romans 1:8, 9; 12:9–21; 15:7, 13).
  Your friend,
  Paul

Think about how friendships could grow in your home, your school, and your community if everyone would work at being the kind of friend Paul describes in this letter! Why not plant some seeds of friendship today?

* Stephen F. Olford, *The Grace of Giving* (Grand Rapids, Mich.: Zondervan Publishing House, 1972), pp. 47, 48.

SHARING GOD

Journal

- Suggest ways to solve friendship problems. Your response might include one or more of the following situations:
  1. How to get better acquainted with someone.
  2. How to help someone who is trying to make friends but is not successful.
  3. How to help a newcomer to your school feel comfortable.

Dig a Little Deeper

1. Reread the exerpts from Paul's letter to his Roman friends and in your own words list seven ways in which he describes what Christian friends do.

2. Decide what you might say to someone who says, "Yes, I've heard that I'm supposed to be friendly to people. But the truth is, I really don't like a lot of the people I know. How am I supposed to be friendly to people I don't like?" Ephesians 4:31, 32

3. When you reach out to be a friend to another person, the Lord always adds a special bonus. Select one of the following paragraphs and then state it in your own words.

   "It is as we give ourselves to God for the service of humanity that He gives Himself to us. No one can give place in his own heart and life for the stream of God's blessings to flow to others, without receiving in himself a rich reward" (*Thoughts From the Mount of Blessing,* p. 81).

   "Speak often words that will be a strength and an inspiration to those who hear. We are altogether too indifferent in regard to one another. We forget that our fellow laborers are often in need of words of hope and cheer. When one is in trouble, call upon him and speak comforting words to him. This is true friendship" (Ellen G. White Comments, *SDA Bible Commentary,* vol. 7, p. 928).

4. The Bible contains many stories of people whose lives demonstrate what it means to be friends. Choose one person from the list below and write what you learn about the person named and how friendship was shown.
   Obadiah: 1 Kings 18:1–4
   A man from Samaria: Luke 10:30–35
   Jonathan: 1 Samuel 20:30–42
   Onesiphorus: 2 Timothy 1:16–18

5. Gossip is a threat to friendship. It is wrong because it hurts someone. The Bible speaks of those who gossip as "talebearers." What does gossip do? Proverbs 16:28; 20:19; 25:23

Activities

A. Read the poem "The Right Kind of People" (see TRM, p. 88).
    Answer the following questions using lines from the poem to support
    your answers:
    1. What sort of people had the traveling packman in verse one left
        behind?
    2. What sort of people had the pilgrim in verse two left behind?
    3. How could one man find one type of people and another man find
        the opposite type of people in the same city?

B. It has been observed that people choose friends who are most like
    themselves. There is also the belief that "opposites attract." Make a "T"
    chart showing in one column your personality traits and in a second
    column the traits of a close friend. Are your friend's traits similar to or
    opposite of yours?

C. As a class, initiate a friendship with an older person in the church that
    you do not know well and plan a special activity with that person. Make
    this a project for the remainder of the school year.

D. Create a classroom chart with the following heading: "The best way to
    destroy an enemy is to make him your friend." List ways this can be
    accomplished.

To Learn More

The Bible Story, vol. 10, pp. 128–131
The Bible Pageant, (1986), vol. 4, pp. 63–67
Joe Wheeler, *Heart to Heart Stories of Friendship* (Review and Herald®
    Publishing Association, 1999).

30

SHARING GOD

"Have the people of Israel build me a holy sanctuary so I can live among them" *(Exodus 25:8).*

Construction workers use a variety of skills when erecting a building. They accurately and carefully fit the pieces together to make the building strong and beautiful. In much the same way, the Holy Spirit fits together believers of all nations, cultures, and ages to form one strong, beautiful building, the dwelling place of God on earth—the church.

What Is a Church?

Acts 9:31

I will bring them to my holy mountain of Jerusalem and fill them with joy in my house of prayer. I will accept their burnt offerings and sacrifices, because my Temple will be called a house of prayer for all nations" (Isaiah 56:7).

In the Old Testament, we read about the sanctuary or the temple or God's house as a place of worship. The word *church* doesn't appear until the New Testament.

What do you remember about the desert sanctuary?

But what is the broadest definition of the word *church*? Consider the words of Jacob in Genesis 28. Jacob had fallen asleep with a stone under his head as a pillow, the usual custom of travelers. During the night, he had a dream in which angels of God were going up and down a stairway or ladder to heaven. At the top of the stairway was God, who gave a blessing and assurance to Jacob. The next morning Jacob said, "'Surely the LORD is in this place, and I wasn't even aware of it!'" (verse 16). He went on to say, "'What an awesome place this is! It is none other than the house of God, the very gateway to heaven!'" (verse 17). Then Jacob used the stone he had employed as a pillow to set up an altar, a memorial pillar. By pouring oil over it, he showed reverence for the place. He called it Bethel, or "house of God."

Jacob sensed God's presence, calling the place the house of God, an awesome place. Others became aware of God's presence when He told them He was there. Think about Moses at the burning bush. God told him to "'take off your sandals, for you are standing on holy ground'" (Exodus 3:5). The church, in its broadest definition, is "wherever God is present." *The church is where we worship God.*

Why do you think it was important to Jacob to build a memorial?

SHARING GOD

In New Testament times, we see this definition expanded to include a group of believers. Matthew makes this clear when he records Jesus' words in describing how He will build His church (Matthew 16:18) and again where he quotes Jesus regarding how a sinning believer should be treated (Matthew 18). In the book of Acts, Luke uses the word *church* to describe the people who followed the teachings of Jesus, the group of believers. In Acts 2:41 he tells about three thousand people believing, being baptized, and being added to the church. Paul's writings also contain references about the church. Nine of his letters were written to specific churches. In his letters he gave encouragement and advice for getting along as individuals within a church.

Do we ever see such large baptisms today?

Just as it was in Paul's time, the church today is a place for people to meet together to encourage one another. It is a place for people who need God's healing from the damage sin has done. It is a place for struggling, growing, sometimes stumbling Christians to find help, friendship, and a deeper understanding of God.

Everyone has problems. People in the church are not exceptions. No one should ever find fault with those who do not always succeed in gaining victories over their shortcomings and failures. Those who are growing into Christ's likeness need to be assured that He is always with them to guide and help them as they grow.

How should we act toward this group of people known as "the church"? With love and encouraging support! In the same way Jesus said in Matthew 7:12, "Do to others whatever you would like them to do to you." The church is not a place for perfect people, but rather for a group of believers seeking to become like Jesus.

The church is like a family—God's family—in which there is a place for everyone. That includes you. The church can give us friendship, support, and a feeling of belonging. And just as in a family, we give, we receive, and we forgive.

Why is forgiveness an important aspect of the church?

But to the growing Christian, the church is even more. Christ Himself has told us so. "Where two or three gather together as my followers, I am there among them" (Matthew 18:20). God is there with us when we seek His presence. *The church, the family of God, is a place of healing, fellowship, and worship.*

Do you remember the story of the Samaritan woman at the well? In her attempt to divert the attention from herself, she asked Jesus if the only right place to worship God was in the temple at Jerusalem or on a mountain near where she lived. His answer startled her when He replied, "'Believe me, dear woman, the time is coming when it will no longer matter whether you worship the Father on this mountain or in Jerusalem. . . . But the time is coming—indeed it's here now—when true worshipers will worship the Father in spirit and in truth'" (John 4:21–23). We worship God when we thoughtfully, honestly, and reverently honor Him.

Jesus' encounter with the woman at the well shows us another aspect of the church. The church is a place where lives are changed, where growth occurs, and where sinful individuals living in a sinful world are given the opportunity to accept the forgiveness and life-changing presence that God can only provide. Because of our gratitude to God, we choose to worship Him. *The church is a place where growth occurs and character is changed.*

We worship God when we respect and enjoy His creation, remembering that He created such things as sights, sounds, smells, flavors, and textures for us to enjoy. We can tell Him that we are thankful for these gifts, and we can show Him our thanks by enjoying them. We worship God when we treat people as Christ treated them. We worship God when we obey Him lovingly and willingly. Genuine worship is an expression of our appreciation, love, and trust in God. Such worship will help us to become more like Him in the way we live every day.

> Moses met God by a burning bush.
> Abraham met Him under the stars and on top of a mountain.
> David met Him as he herded sheep among the hills.
> John met Him on a lonely island.
> Cleopas met Him on a country road.
> You can meet Him, too, at any time, in any place.
> And wherever you choose to meet Him is a place of worship,
>> a holy place.

SHARING GOD

Journal

- How do you benefit from the church? What could you do for the church?

Dig a Little Deeper

1. Define *church*? Use the narrative, a dictionary, thesaurus, Bible dictionary, and/or concordance.

2. We worship God when we treat others as Christ did. With this statement in mind, complete the following sentences:
   a. I should treat my church leaders . . . (1 Thessalonians 5:12, 13)
   b. I should meet with other church members because . . . (Hebrews 10:23–25)
   c. I can share my faith by . . . (Romans 15:1, 2)

3. Each of the following references tells us something about the attitudes that are part of genuine worship. Write the words that describe the attitude you think the writer of each psalm was expressing.
   a. Psalm 16:11
   b. Psalm 18:1
   c. Psalm 40:8
   d. Psalm 51:1–4
   e. Psalm 128:1
   f. Psalm 150

4. Use Internet sources or an encyclopedia to find a diagram of a cathedral. Compare the arrangement of the space and the furnishings with those of your church. What aspects of your church give you a feeling of worship?

Activities

A. Invite your pastor or another church leader to talk about how students fit into the life of the church. As a group, make a list of questions that you would like to have your pastor answer. Give the list to the pastor in advance of the visit.

B. The Scriptures contain many wonderful references and promises regarding the church. Use a concordance and the narrative to find some of these. Select three and make attractive bookmarks with the texts you choose. Share them with someone who is not a member of your church.

C. Create a flyer that could be used to promote the programs and services of the church.

D. The church gives people an opportunity to praise and worship the Lord. Memorize Psalm 150 and present it as a special selection at your weekly chapel service, Sabbath School program, or church service.

To Learn More

Ephesians 2:19–22
The Acts of the Apostles, chaps. 1; 2; 58

Memory Verse

"Don't let anyone think less of you because you are young. Be an example to all believers in what you say, in the way you live, in your love, your faith, and your purity" (1 Timothy 4:12).

Like the lights of a city built on a hill, the influence of one Christian young person, one Christian home, one Christian school or church, cannot be hidden. Ellen White once wrote to a group of leaders, "You must take broader views," she advised. "Your house is the world" (*Life Sketches*, p. 209). What do you think she meant? In what way is your house the world?

Your House Is the World

Matthew 5:14–16

The world in which Jesus lived was filled with problems much like many of those in our world today: wars, violence, cruelty, prejudice, crime, intolerance, poverty, and hatred. Jesus was not indifferent to these great problems. His way of dealing with them was to apply the only lasting remedy there is for a world filled with sin and misery. His way was to demonstrate God's love in His life, so people could be changed into His likeness. That task He has passed on to us.

"I am giving you a new commandment: Love each other. Just as I have loved you, you should love each other. Your love for one another will prove to the world that you are my disciples" (John 13:34, 35). The kind of love Jesus is talking about is not just a warm feeling down deep in our hearts. His kind of love is something we do. Loving others as Jesus does means being concerned about people no matter who they are, what they do, or where they live. It means giving our time and our energy to people who need help. It means being sympathetic to people who are going through grief and loss. It means being kind to people who need a friend, even to those who may be unpopular or irritating.

The Lord gave Ellen White a great vision of what young people can do as their special part in spreading the good news about God's love to the world. She expressed it in these words: "With such an army of workers as our youth, rightly trained, might furnish, how soon the message of a crucified, risen, and soon-coming Saviour might be carried to the whole world! How soon might the end come—the end of suffering and sorrow and sin!" (*Education*, p. 271).

Think of the young student missionaries and Task Force workers who gladly postpone a year in college to volunteer to help spread the good news of God's never-ending love. They go wherever the need is the greatest, regardless of how lonely the place or how difficult the work may be. Young people involved in mission projects or in youth groups such as the Pathfinder Club play an important role in sharing the message of Jesus' love to their communities and neighborhoods.

How do you think young people can share God's love?

Jamal Franklyn preached his first sermon at the age of seven on Pathfinder Day at Advent Avenue, his home church in Barbados. Then in 2001, he participated in Mission 2000 and Beyond, a ministry begun by the children's department leaders to involve young people in evangelism. As a result, fourteen people were baptized.

In 2003 Jamal and other young people went to Saint Vincent for two weeks, where they conducted evangelistic meetings and community-service projects that included visiting people in the community and cleaning streets and beaches. During the crusade, many youth evangelists preached—one as young as ten years of age. Twenty-two people were baptized. In 2004 similar missionary outreach was conducted in Dominica with eight baptized, and in 2005 twenty-three were baptized in Saint Lucia. Every year young people from Barbados go to other countries to sing, preach, witness, and share God's love.

Jamal states that he has dedicated his life to ministry "because there are people out there who want the word of God, people out there who want to have the same joy, the same peace, the same love—everything that I've found in Jesus Christ." When Jamal is not preaching or on mission trips, he is engaged in ministry at school because "ministry is something that you live every day."[1]

How do your friends see Jesus in you?

Academy and college students in Missouri and Colorado spread God's love through literature evangelism. During the summer of 2006, young people in Missouri visited nearly one hundred thousand homes in St. Louis and Springfield. Not only did they sell truth-filled literature, they also signed people up for Revelation seminars, stop-smoking programs, cooking schools, and Bible studies. In Denver, academy students visited 99,000 homes selling Adventist literature and offering Bible-study request cards. These and other students are playing a major role in Mid-America Union Conference's five-year goal of reaching every one of its nearly twenty-five million residents through some form of evangelistic outreach.[2]

Adventist Community Team Services (ACTS), an ongoing Adventist disaster relief organization based in the Southern Union Conference, is much like most other relief groups. Its volunteers help disaster victims by supplying them with food, water, blankets, and other basic necessities. They cut down trees and clear debris after hurricanes devastate a town. And they provide emotional encouragement to those who have lost most, sometimes all, of their possessions. But there is one big difference—almost all ACTS volunteers are youth and young adults.

In August 2005, Hurricane Katrina damaged 95 percent of the buildings at Bass Memorial Academy, located near Hattiesburg, Mississippi. ACTS was called to help. While on their way, the ACTS team contacted Southern Adventist and Andrews universities, asking for more volunteers. Both schools agreed to help. Using generators for power, the students stripped roofs, gutted classrooms, and cut up trees. They also set up a distribution center to provide food, water, and ice for the academy staff and students as well as the surrounding community. As word got out about what they were doing, more than six hundred carloads of hurricane victims came to the site every day to receive aid.

More help was needed, and before long academy and college students from across the United States arrived in Mississippi. Then, at the request of the Red Cross and the State Emergency Operations Center, ACTS expanded their operation to Waveland, Mississippi, where many survivors had lost homes, cars, and jobs. ACTS provided hot meals every day for more than six thousand people. Water, food, ice, and clothes were given to people who arrived daily in up to one thousand cars.

"There were so many chances to share God with needy people," remarked Eric McKay, a student at Heritage Academy in Tennessee. "It was just so amazing to see what God can do for a devastated town through a huge group of students pumped and ready to work for Christ," added Jolene Shafer, also a Heritage Academy student. "I have never felt like I was used more by Christ."[3]

You may not be able to travel far from home to work for Christ. How can you volunteer for Him right where you live?

Elementary and middle school students at Olney Adventist Preparatory School in Maryland organized a variety of projects to raise over five thousand dollars to sponsor gifts they selected from the Adventist Development and

SHARING GOD

Relief Agency International's (ADRA) annual gift catalog. Every gift in ADRA's catalog benefits people around the world in ways that provide not only immediate, tangible help, but also dignity and hope for the future.

In the center of Russia, ADRA is helping to nurture and care for street children and orphans. The things they need most are warm food, clothing, shoes, regular medical checkups, and education, and just one dollar provides all the care one child needs for one day. Students in the third and fourth grade chose to sponsor this project. They raised over two thousand dollars by participating in a walk/runathon, doing extra chores like cleaning, dusting, and vacuuming, and giving money they had saved.

Students in the upper grades also participated in the walk/runathon. Their classes chose to buy goats, cows, chickens, and sheep for needy families in Ethiopia, Zimbabwe, and other countries in Africa. Milk, eggs, wool, and other products these animals produce provide food and clothing that can be used by the families or sold to earn income.[4]

Many other schools across North America are involved each year in various ADRA projects.

Would you like your class to sponsor an ADRA project?

Think about what your part can be to demonstrate God's love. You may think, "Who, me? What can I do? I'm only one person, I can never make a difference." WRONG! You can make a difference. A big difference. You can say:

> I am only one,
> But still I am one.
> I cannot do everything,
> But still I can do something;
> And because I cannot do everything
> I will not refuse to do the something that I can do.
> —Edward Everett Hale

Your part may certainly include such things as inviting people to church, being able to explain what we believe, and giving offerings to help spread the gospel around the world. But there is an even more important way in which you can do your part. More than anything else, God needs you to reveal His character by the unselfish, thoughtful things you do to help others. God wants to be made known through His people—through those who depend on God's strength and are being changed into His likeness. And that includes you. Wherever you are, whatever you do, your "house" is the world.

"You are the light of the world. . . . Let your good deeds shine" (Matthew 5:14–16).

1. Omar Bourne, "Called to Minister," *Adventist World*—NAD, September 2006, pp. 16–19.

2. Martin Weber, "America's Heartland—Adventists' Opportunity," *Adventist World*—NAD, December 2006, pp. 26–29.

3. Jim Ingersoll, "ACTS of God," *Adventist Review*, December 14, 2006, pp. 18, 19.

4. Kid's View, *Adventist Review*, December 28, 2006.

SHARING GOD

Journal

- What can you do to let your light shine? How can you make a difference in someone else's life?

Dig a Little Deeper

1. Letting one's light shine includes both actions and words. Find at least three things Christians may do to let their light shine. Matthew 25:34–40; Isaiah 58:7

2. Where will Christians let their light shine? Acts 1:8; Matthew 24:14; Luke 8:38, 39

3. Luke describes the apostles as a group of Christians who lived such unselfish lives of service that the whole community knew about it. Make a list of the things they did and the result of their actions. Acts 2:43–47

4. Jesus says a Christian should be a lightbearer. Explain what this means in terms of how a Christian will act. Matthew 5:14–16

5. Reread the paragraph in this lesson taken from the book *Education*, page 271. What do you think the words "rightly trained" mean? In what ways are Christian young people like an "army"?

6. Give some biblical examples of young people whose lives would have qualified them for membership in such an "army." Tell why you would include them.

Activities

A. Search through recent copies of the *Adventist Review* and other church papers for something being done to spread the good news about God. Prepare a report to be given to the class.

B. Create a collage. Use a large sheet of poster board or cardboard from a packing box cut into a circle to represent the globe. Collect pictures of people from many areas around the world. Cover both sides of the circle with these pictures. Give the collage a title that emphasizes the topic of this lesson, such as a phrase from Matthew 28:19, 20. Hang the collage in such a way that it can rotate freely to show both sides.

C. Name three specific things students in grades five through eight can do to help someone in need. Select one thing you can do, make a plan for carrying it out, and then actually do it.

D. Can you imagine what Jesus would do today if He were walking among us here on earth? Imagine that you are a newspaper reporter assigned the task of following Jesus for twenty-four hours. You have just completed the assignment and returned home. Write an article on what He has been doing.

To Learn More

www.adra.org
www.adventistmission.org
www.communityservices.org
www.maranatha.org

As you have responded to the working of the Holy Spirit in your life, you have been preparing for the greatest event in earth's history, the second coming of Christ. Let Jesus lead you toward this marvelous occasion as you continue to become like Him.

unit 7

BECOMING LIKE HIM

While You're Studying

BECOMING LIKE HIM

A Write the memory verses for the unit and add them to your file.

B As a class, make a timeline depicting the events of Jesus' life.

C As a class, produce a play on the Second Coming. Divide your class into groups to do the following: (1) write a script, (2) record appropriate music, (3) make or find necessary props. Consider presenting this play as an end of the year activity.

D As a culminating activity for the unit, publish a newspaper covering the topics that were studied. Your paper could include feature articles about each of the lessons, artwork, an advice column, letters to the editor, photos, an editorial, or poetry.

© DARREL TANK

Memory Verse

"'Do to others whatever you would like them to do to you. This is the essence of all that is taught in the law and the prophets'" (Matthew 7:12).

Jesus told stories, preached sermons, drew word pictures, scolded hypocrites, blessed His listeners, offered prayers, and prophesied future events. He lived in a society that was different from yours. He lived during a time that was different from yours. He spoke a language that was different from yours. Is there anything He said that would be relevant to you today?

And Jesus Said . . .

Matthew 5–7; 18:21–35; 22:15–22
Luke 10:30–37

God's chosen people were to provide a vista of His love to the entire world. His followers were to reveal His love and His plan to all humanity. . . . [But] for generations the Israelites repeated a cycle of apostasy, repentance, reformation, apostasy, repentance, reformation, until they were taken captive by heathen kings."*

When the Hebrews returned to their homes from captivity, they were anxious to not fall into the same cycle of apostasy as their ancestors had. Afraid other nations would contaminate them, they shut themselves off from everyone. Believing they were superior to other people, they kept the Scriptures to themselves.

As the time approached for the fulfillment of Isaiah's prophecy of the promised Messiah, the Hebrew people were suffering under the oppression of Roman rule. God's people were waiting for a Messiah, not to rescue them from spiritual darkness, but to overthrow the tyranny of the Romans. Thus, the Israelites, as a nation, were not prepared for the words Jesus had to say.

And Jesus said a great deal about many things. He talked to crowds of people, such as the time He preached the Sermon on the Mount. He talked to small groups of people, such as when He gave instructions to His disciples. And He talked to individuals, such as Nicodemus, who came to Him when no one else was around.

Whether talking to one person or talking to many, Jesus had interesting and often controversial things to say—like the time Peter came to Jesus and asked Him how often one should forgive someone who sins against you. Peter felt he was being very gracious when he suggested seven times. " 'No, not seven times,' Jesus replied, 'but seventy times seven!' " (Matthew 18:22). To forgive someone when they have wronged you is hard, but to forgive them over and over without keeping track seems impossible, but this is just what Jesus asked us to do.

BECOMING LIKE HIM

Jesus didn't just ask us to forgive others; He showed us how to forgive. When Jesus was arrested and taken to be tried by Caiaphas, John and Peter followed the procession to Caiaphas's home. In the courtyard, as Peter was warming himself by the fire, he denied that he even knew Jesus. Three times Peter denied Jesus. And then the rooster crowed. Peter felt so ashamed. He turned and looked at Jesus only to see the look of intense love in His eyes.

Often Jesus gave advice that His hearers found difficult to accept. Take the rich young ruler. He came to Jesus asking what he could do to be saved. Jesus, knowing the man's attraction to material goods, asked him to sell all he owned and give it to the poor. Sadly, the young ruler turned away from Jesus, for he was very rich.

But many people did listen to Him. Crowds of people followed Him, not only to see His miracles but also to listen to His words. They came because Jesus spoke directly to the problems in their lives. What He said speaks to our lives too.

Take taxes, for example. Taxes are a problem for people today. Taxes were perhaps even more of a problem in Jesus' day. Taxes took money people needed for other things, and they were paid to a foreign power. Palestine was occupied by Caesar's armies, whom the people hated. They also hated the tax collectors, some of whom were Jews.

One day some of the Pharisees and Herodians plotted together to trick Jesus. They asked Him if they should pay taxes. If Jesus said No, He would anger the government. If He said Yes, He would anger the people. Instead of answering directly, Jesus asked for a coin, called their attention to Caesar's portrait on the coin, and said, " 'Give to Caesar what belongs to Caesar, and give to God what belongs to God' " (Matthew 22:21).

In addition to paying taxes, what else do we owe to our government and community?

Another example is discrimination. It is a problem today, just as it was in Jesus' day. Not only the Jewish leaders, but also Jesus' own disciples, discriminated against children, women, Samaritans, Gentiles, tax collectors, and even a preacher not of their group who was casting out devils in Jesus' name.

By word and action, Jesus demonstrated total acceptance of others. He said, " 'Let the children come to me' " (Mark 10:14). He started a conversation with a Samaritan woman and accepted women as His followers. He said of the Roman centurion, " 'I tell you the truth, I haven't seen faith like this in all

Israel!'" (Matthew 8:10). He went on to say that many who were not Israelites would be saved, and some of those who were Israelites would be lost. He said to Levi Matthew, the tax collector, "'Follow me and be my disciple'" (Matthew 9:9). And to Zacchaeus, another tax collector, "'Quick, come down! I must be a guest in your home today'" (Luke 19:5). To His disciple John, who was angry about someone casting out devils in Jesus' name, He said, "'Anyone who is not against us is for us'" (Mark 9:40). Jesus did not judge anyone by age, race, gender, or occupation.

Jesus had a great deal to say about our love for God and the way we treat one another. One day a Pharisee, an expert in the law, asked Jesus, "'Teacher, which is the most important commandment in the law of Moses?'" (Matthew 22:36).

The expert continued his question by asking, "'And who is my neighbor?'" (Luke 10:29). In reply, Jesus told the parable of the good Samaritan (Luke 10:30–37). In the parable a priest and a Levite passed by a wounded man, but the Samaritan stopped to help him. Jesus turned around the question from "'Who is my neighbor?'" to "'Which of these three would you say was a neighbor to the man who was attacked by bandits?'" When the expert in the law admitted it was the Samaritan, Jesus told him to go and do likewise.

Who is your neighbor?

Jesus also spoke words of comfort. To Jairus, whose daughter was dying, Jesus said, "'Don't be afraid. Just have faith, and she will be healed'" (Luke 8:50). To the storm that the disciples feared would sink the boat they were in, Jesus said, "'Silence! Be still!'" (Mark 4:39). To the paralyzed man who had been let down through the roof, He said, "'My child, your sins are forgiven'" (Mark 2:5). And to Lazarus, who was dead and had been three days in the tomb, Jesus said, "'Lazarus, come out!'" (John 11:43). So powerful were Jesus' words that, to the amazement of all who were watching, Lazarus came out of the tomb.

Jesus' words have the same power today.

Can you think of some examples that demonstrate the power of Jesus' words?

* *God Is the Victor*, p. 143.

BECOMING LIKE HIM

Journal

- This lesson is about things Jesus said while He lived on earth.
  Write some of His words that especially speak to you and explain why.

Dig a Little Deeper

1. Even after Jesus' resurrection, the disciples still showed some prejudice against Gentiles. Peter had a vision concerning this. Tell the vision in your own words and explain what it means. Acts 10:9–29

2. Read Matthew 5:43–6:8. List three things Jesus said that might apply to your life and tell how they could apply.

3. Read the story of the sheep and the goats in Matthew 25:31–46
   a. Who is represented by the king? the sheep? the goats?
   b. What did Jesus use as the basis for separating the sheep from the goats?
   c. How do you know that both the sheep and the goats were surprised at what the king said they had done or not done?
   d. Explain in your own words what Jesus means by the saying, " 'I tell you the truth, when you did it to one of the least of these my brothers and sisters, you were doing it to me!' "

4. After Jesus' resurrection, Peter applied the "give to Caesar" principle when dealing with the authorities. What part of the principle did he apply? Acts 5:27–29

5. What three things did Jesus say about forgiveness? Matthew 6:12–15

6. List the steps Jesus said Christians should follow in settling a difference. Matthew 18:15–17

7. The desire to be first or the greatest is prevalent in our world today.
   a. How did Jesus define greatness? Matthew 18:1–4; 23:11, 12
   b. Do you think it is wrong to desire to be first or the best? Explain.

8. Sometimes it is difficult to follow Jesus' teachings in today's society. Find in any four of the following Bible texts a phrase or clause that might help you. Psalm 119:11; Philippians 4:13; 2 Corinthians 12:9; Zechariah 4:6; 1 Corinthians 15:57; Jude 24

Activities

A. If Jesus were living on earth today, He would probably tell parables that include modern-day things such as cars, computers, space shuttles, et cetera. Write a modern-day parable that would teach one of the same lessons as in the narrative.

B. Look up the word *denarius* in a Bible commentary or dictionary or on the Internet. Prepare a report on the coins or types of money that may have been used in Jesus' time. Try to determine their equivalent in today's currency.

C. Choose any single statement that Jesus made. Illustrate the thought with a poster and print the quotation on it.

D. Plan a project to help others. You may wish to work with classmates in making these plans.

To Learn More

Matthew 5–7
The Bible Pageant (1986), vol. 4, pp. 102–114
The Bible Story, vol. 10, pp. 132–134
Thoughts From the Mount of Blessing

33

Memory Verse

"He went a little farther and bowed with his face to the ground, praying, 'My Father! If it is possible, let this cup of suffering be taken away from me. Yet I want your will to be done, not mine'" (Matthew 26:39).

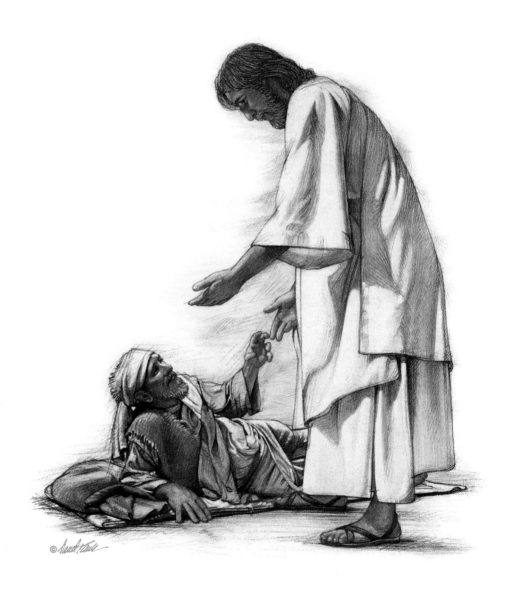

"Actions speak louder than words" is a proverb used to show that what you do is more important than what you say. When people are honest, their actions give the same message as their words. Jesus demonstrated this principle in His life. His behavior was consistent with His teachings.

What other characteristics did Jesus demonstrate in His life?

To Do as He Did

Matthew, Mark, Luke, and John

Terry Fox was eighteen years old and a student at Simon Fraser University in British Columbia when he was diagnosed as having a rare form of bone cancer and had to have a leg amputated. He determined to be strong in spite of his handicap. Since he was a student in physical and health education, he trained strenuously for two and a half years before undertaking the first one-legged run across Canada. Unfortunately, after completing 5,000 kilometers (3,000 mi) of the approximately 8,000 kilometers (4,800 mi) that span the width of Canada, he succumbed to the dreaded disease of cancer and died on June 28, 1981.

Three years later Steve Fonyo, then eighteen himself and another one-legged cancer victim, began the same trek at the same location—the St. John's Harbour in Newfoundland on the Atlantic Ocean. Steve had lost his leg when he was twelve years old. Depressed, discouraged, and bald because of chemotherapy, he dropped out of school in grade ten. But Steve determined to complete the run that Terry had begun. On March 31, 1984, Steve began by dipping his artificial leg in the Atlantic Ocean. He collected some Atlantic water and fourteen months later, on May 29, 1985, he dipped his artificial leg and poured the Atlantic water into the Pacific Ocean at the Strait of Juan de Fuca off the coast of British Columbia.

Between these two young men, millions of dollars have been raised for cancer research in Canada. Both said: "We are determined to . . . ," and both lives demonstrated that determination. Both planned, organized, and arranged for years before embarking on their project. Both had strong convictions that they should make a contribution to society—to help ease the pain of loss due to cancer. Both stood firm for what they believed. Today "Terry Fox Runs" are still held!

From the time of His birth, Jesus was under attack from Satan. Without God's protection, He would have been killed by Herod while He was still a

BECOMING LIKE HIM

baby. Although His earthly parents loved Him dearly, as He grew, Jesus was not always accepted by His older brothers, Joseph's sons.

At the age of twelve Jesus openly demonstrated the path His life would take. He would speak with authority and complete the work He had come to earth to do. This would take great courage, determination, trustworthiness, and compassion.

At some point as He was growing up, Jesus realized who He was and why He was on earth. In the temple He said He must be about His Father's business. Before that time, through study and the work of the Holy Spirit, Jesus came to the realization that He was the Messiah. Imagine reading the words of Isaiah and realizing they were describing you.

How did Jesus come to realize who He was and what work He was to do on earth?

"He was despised and rejected—a man of sorrows, acquainted with deepest grief. We turned our backs on him and looked the other way. He was despised, and we did not care. Yet it was our weakness he carried; it was our sorrows that weighed him down. And we thought his troubles were a punishment from God, a punishment for his own sins! But he was pierced for our rebellion, crushed for our sins. He was beaten so we could be whole. He was whipped so we could be healed. All of us, like sheep, have strayed away. We have left God's paths to follow our own. Yet the LORD laid on him the sins of us all" (Isaiah 53:3–6).

Imagine watching the sacrificial system in the temple and knowing that you are the Lamb of God. We don't know how Jesus felt when He first became aware of who He was and what He must do. We do know Jesus accepted His mission and never wavered from it.

Later, when Jesus tried to tell His disciples that He would die, they lacked the courage to accept or believe what Jesus recognized as a teenager. Because they could not face this reality, they were totally shattered when His death came.

Can you think of an incident when Jesus tried to tell His disciples about His death but they wouldn't listen?

Following His baptism, Jesus went into the wilderness to fast and pray. When He was weak and tired, Satan appeared to Him as an angel of light. Three times Satan tempted Jesus, but Jesus never yielded to the temptation. Among the temptations that Satan used was one to avoid the very work that Jesus had come to do. Satan showed Jesus in an instant all the kingdoms of the world and said to Jesus, "I will give you the glory of these kingdoms and authority over them . . . because they are mine to give to anyone I please. I will give it all to you if you will worship me" (Luke 4:6, 7). Jesus knew that Satan was lying. He knew that this seemingly easy way to regain the world was not God's plan. He knew what must be done to save us, and He would do His Father's will.

After Jesus began teaching and healing, He was harassed by religious leaders. At times He confronted the "important people" of the day. His followers must have sometimes wondered why He did not try to avoid conflict. Upsetting the money tables in the temple and healing people on the Sabbath day upset the priests. Calling religious leaders a "brood of snakes" was not the way to win goodwill. There were places in Palestine where Jesus was dearly loved. Crowds of people would welcome Him. However, Jesus did not limit Himself to these areas. When His enemies tried to kill Him, Jesus would go to these safer places for a little while because He knew His work was not yet finished. But Jesus would return to confront His enemies. Being accepted and staying alive were not what motivated Jesus' actions. Doing His Father's will and finishing His mission to save us were. Jesus spent many hours in prayer asking for His Father's help in living His life.

Why do you think the things Jesus did upset the Jewish leaders?

It wasn't that Jesus didn't care what happened to Him. During the final hours of His life as He was facing arrest, torture, and death, Jesus prayed three times, "'My Father! If it is possible, let this cup of suffering be taken away from me.'" But He added, "'Yet I want your will to be done, not mine'" (Matthew 26:39). This prayer was not answered with a Yes. And Jesus went to meet those who would kill Him.

How do we know it wasn't always easy for Jesus to do what He knew He must do?

Almost the last words Jesus spoke before He died were, "'It is finished!'"

(John 19:30). He had never once swerved from the mission He recognized while He was still very young.

That Sabbath as He rested in the tomb and His friends and disciples grieved, they remembered Him not only for His steadfastness and courage but also for His love and care for individuals.

Nicodemus remembered how he had come to Jesus secretly at night because he did not want anyone to know he had spoken to Jesus. Jesus had kept this secret. But the day before, Nicodemus had at last declared he was a disciple of Jesus. He had gone with Joseph of Arimathea to request the body of Jesus so it could be buried properly (John3:1, 2; 19:38, 39).

Jesus' mother, Mary, remembered that even while Jesus was suffering on the cross, He thought of her needs and asked the disciple John to care for her (John 19:26, 27).

Mary Magdalene remembered that Jesus had cast seven devils from her heart and mind. He had lifted her from despair and ruin. He had praised her for her gift of sweet-smelling ointment when Judas had condemned its cost (Luke 7:36–50; Mark 14:3–9).

The widow of Nain remembered how Jesus had stopped the funeral procession and raised her son from the dead (Luke 7:11–17).

And the disciples remembered how patient Jesus had been with them. Many times they had been difficult and slow to understand. They had not listened when Jesus tried to tell them how His life would end. Even now they were in despair, not remembering, not believing He would live again.

How did the disciples misunderstand Jesus?

Jesus does live. Our hope and faith are based on the fact that He was resurrected from the dead. The record of Jesus' life on earth tells us what kind of Person will return to take us to heaven. Forty days after His resurrection, Jesus' followers were gathered on a mountain. After Jesus spoke to them, He was slowly taken up to heaven. As a cloud hid Him from their sight, they must have stood there with mouths open, incredulous looks on their faces. Two angels appeared to them and said, "Men of Galilee . . . why are you standing here staring into heaven? Jesus has been taken from you into heaven, but someday He will return from heaven the same way as you saw him go!" (Acts 1:11).

This same Jesus will come for you!

BECOMING LIKE HIM

Journal

- How do you seek God's help to live a Christian life?

Dig a Little Deeper

1. Where did Jesus get the help He needed to accomplish His work on earth? Matthew 14:23; Luke 6:12

2. Throughout His ministry Jesus demonstrated both wisdom and courage. Read John 10:22–11:16.
   a. Why did He go back across the Jordan?
   b. What did the people across the Jordan think about Jesus?
   c. What caused Jesus to return to Judea?
   d. How did the disciples feel about Jesus going back to Judea?
   e. What did Thomas say about going? What does this statement say about Thomas?

3. Nicodemus and a friend were secret disciples of Jesus. John 19:38–40
   a. What was the friend's name?
   b. What special service did they render to Jesus after His death?

4. Four characteristics of Jesus (courage, wisdom, steadfastness, and compassion) were discussed in this lesson. From what you have discussed this year and what you know about Jesus' life, list at least four other characteristics and give an example of each. (If you need a clue, see Lessons 4 and 32.) Identify which of these characteristics you wish to emulate in your own life.

Activities

A. In small groups, construct a diorama showing one of the incidents in which Jesus did something that must have seemed unusual to the people of His day.

B. Use pictures, drawings, Bible texts and/or poetry to make a collage of events in Jesus' life that illustrate one of the following characteristics: (1) courage, (2) compassion, (3) patience, (4) wisdom.

C. Research symbols used in the Bible for the Messiah. Cut paper to make a mosaic illustrating the symbols.

D. Prepare a monologue, dialogue, or reader's theater of Jesus' life. This could be an individual or cooperative assignment. Check with your Sabbath School superintendent about presenting this as part of a Sabbath School program.

To Learn More

The Bible Pageant (1986), vol. 4, pp. 44–46
The Desire of Ages
Messiah

BECOMING LIKE HIM

Memory Verse

"'Look, I am coming soon, bringing my reward with me to repay all people according to their deeds. I am the Alpha and the Omega, the First and the Last, the Beginning and the End.'" "He who is the faithful witness to all these things says, 'Yes, I am coming soon!'" (Revelation 22:12, 13, 20).

We spend a great deal of time waiting. We wait in lines, wait for Christmas and birthdays, and wait for vacations. For centuries, beginning with Adam and Eve, people waited for the Messiah. Now we wait for His return. What are you waiting for? What can you expect?

The Promise

Revelation 21; 22

Long before He created our world, Jesus had a plan to redeem us. When Adam and Eve chose sin over obedience, He revealed the plan to them. For nearly four thousand years, men and women waited and watched for the Messiah to come. They offered sacrifices pointing to the Lamb of God. And God offered salvation to any who would accept. The hope of a coming Messiah changed lives.

The Messiah did come just as He had promised, but not as people expected. He came as a baby welcomed by shepherds and wise men. He came to change lives and offer salvation. As He gathered His disciples, He offered them a new way of life.

Peter, Andrew, James, and John fished when the weather permitted and mended nets when it didn't. Jesus taught them to become fishers of people. Mary Magdalene continually fell into sin's clutches until Jesus offered her freedom, from both her embarrassing lifestyle and the guilt of her choices. Jesus changed lives as He healed the lame, the blind, the deaf, the sick, the lepers. More important, He gave them hope for the present and for the future as they accepted the gift of salvation He offered them.

Jesus continues to change the lives of those who will allow Him to. He offers hope for the present and the future to those who are willing to put their faith in Him. The same life-changing power that turned rugged fishermen into evangelists can change your life. The same love and forgiveness that transformed Mary can bring peace to you. The hope that has inspired God's followers for centuries can give you a purpose and direction. God loves you and wants you to be with Him throughout eternity. He promises to lead your life now and to return so you can live forever in a once-again perfect creation.

As Jesus met with His disciples in the upper room to celebrate the Passover, He washed their feet, ate with them, and talked with them about the future.

BECOMING LIKE HIM

"Simon Peter asked, 'Lord where are you going?' And Jesus replied, 'You can't go with me now, but you will follow me later'" (John 13:36). Jesus went on to say in John 14:1–4: "'Don't let your hearts be troubled. Trust in God, and trust also in me. There is more than enough room in my Father's home. If this were not so, would I have told you that I am going to prepare a place for you? When everything is ready, I will come and get you, so that you will always be with me where I am. And you know the way to where I am going.'"

When Jesus returned to His Father in heaven, angels assured the disciples that He would return. Jesus was taken up into a cloud, and the disciples could no longer see Him. "As they strained to see him rising into heaven, two white-robed men suddenly stood among them. 'Men of Galilee,' they said, 'why are you standing here staring into heaven? Jesus has been taken from you into heaven, but someday he will return from heaven in the same way you have seen him go!'" (Acts 1:10, 11).

Through the power of the Holy Spirit, these disciples spread the message of Jesus to the world. John most likely lived longer than the other disciples. His later years were spent on the Isle of Patmos, a barren volcanic island ten miles (seventeen kilometers) by six miles (ten kilometers) in the Aegean Sea. Some of John's enemies decided that the island, used as a prison colony by the Romans, would be the perfect place for him. What harm could he do? But even here, John shared the good news of salvation. Even on a deserted prison island, he received messages from heaven. "The sky [will roll] up like a scroll" (Revelation 6:14), and "the Lord himself will come down from heaven with a commanding shout, with the voice of the archangel, and with the trumpet call of God. First, the Christians who have died will rise from their graves" (1 Thessalonians 4:16). Powerful angels will gather God's people "from all over the world—from the farthest ends of the earth and heaven" (Matthew 24:31). A vast throng of beings will fill the heavens in that day. There will be "all the angels," "thousands and millions of angels" (Matthew 25:31; Revelation 5:11), as well as all the people who are redeemed, a great multitude beginning with Adam. There will be so many people that it would seem impossible to count them. They will come from "every nation and tribe and people and language" (Revelation 7:9). In the center of this scene will be Jesus.

What do you think it will be like when Jesus comes?

"Then I saw a new heaven and a new earth, for the old heaven and the old earth had disappeared. And the sea was also gone. And I saw the holy city, the new Jerusalem, coming down from God out of heaven like a bride beautifully dressed for her husband.

"I heard a loud shout from the throne, saying 'Look, God's home is now among his people! He will live with them, and they will be his people. God himself will be with them. He will wipe every tear from their eyes, and there will be no more death or sorrow or crying or pain. All these things are done forever.'

"And the one sitting on the throne said, 'Look I am making everything new!' And then he said to me, 'Write this down, for what I tell you is trustworthy and true'" (Revelation 21:1–5).

Revelation 21 goes on to describe an unimaginable city with streets of pure gold, yet clear as glass, with gates each made of a single huge pearl, with the foundations made of twelve beautiful precious stones including sapphire, emerald, amethyst, and jasper.

After showing John the crystal river flowing from God's throne, the angel instructed him, "Everything you have heard and seen is trustworthy and true. The Lord God, who inspires his prophets, has sent his angel to tell his servants what will happen soon" (Revelation 22:6). Jesus spoke to John saying, "Look, I am coming soon! Blessed are those who obey the words of prophecy written in this book" (Revelation 22:7).

Jesus had given the invitation earlier when He told about the final judgment, "'Come, you who are blessed by my Father, inherit the Kingdom prepared for you from the creation of the world'" (Matthew 25:34). He has continually reminded us of His love and invitation.

What do you expect to find in heaven? When would you want Jesus to come?

Some people are not sure they want Jesus to come—not now anyway. Maybe when they are older and have experienced life—after they've owned a car, had a successful career, traveled, fallen in love, and married. Maybe then they would want Jesus to come. Somehow they feel that if Jesus comes before they have lived all of life, they will be cheated. What they don't realize is that when we actually see Jesus, nothing else will matter anymore. All the good things we want, as well as all the bad things that have happened to us, just aren't important when Jesus comes.

- The emptiness that couldn't be filled when your parents divorced will be gone forever.

BECOMING LIKE HIM

- The loss you felt when your grandparent or mother or father or brother or sister died will no longer be felt.
- The scars that sin has left on your body will be erased.

When the King, our Redeemer and Friend, returns, nothing will matter anymore.

Suddenly we realize that everything we have previously experienced—all the love, the joy, and the happiness we have had—is nothing in comparison to the life God will give us. It will be like a story just beginning, with every page better than the previous. And there is Jesus welcoming us home!

Why does nothing matter anymore when Jesus comes?

The invitation is for you. God invites you into eternity. He wants to wash away the sin and guilt of this world and give you hope of a better one. "Heaven is a good place. I long to be there and behold my lovely Jesus, who gave His life for me, and be changed into His glorious image. Oh, for language to express the glory of the bright world to come! I thirst for the living streams that make glad the city of our God" (*Early Writings*, p. 39).

Earlier this year we talked about justification—salvation from the penalty of sin, and sanctification—salvation from the power of sin. This lesson describes what will happen when we are taken away from this world and all the evil effects of sin are gone. We can call this third kind of salvation, glorification. Three kinds of salvation. Three gifts from God. The first two we can have now. The third we will receive when Jesus comes. Let's be ready to say with John the disciple,

"AMEN! COME, LORD JESUS!"

BECOMING LIKE HIM

Journal

- Reflect on one of the worst things and one of the most exciting things that have happened to you on this earth. Explain how heaven will be different. Then write out your plan for the first hundred years in heaven.

Dig a Little Deeper

1. Jesus spoke frequently about His return to this earth.
   a. Whom did Jesus say would see Him when He comes? Matthew 24:30
   b. When did Jesus say He would come? Matthew 24:36
   c. What promise did Jesus make about His coming? John 14:1–3

2. Jesus told about His second coming. In your own words, tell what He wants us to learn from the following stories.
   a. The parable of the ten virgins. Matthew 25:1–13
   b. The sheep and the goats. Matthew 25:31–46

3. In your own words, state what Jesus said about the commitment of our lives to Him. Matthew 10:32, 33, 37–39

4. What promise is made to those who have had great troubles in this world? Revelation 7:14–17

5. Describe how Jesus looked when He appeared in vision to the disciple John on Patmos. Revelation 1:12–16

6. List five important ideas about the New Jerusalem and the second coming of Jesus. Revelation 21 and 22

Activities

A. Based on the Bible and the writings of Ellen White, write a description of the joyous event, the second coming of Christ. Choose a way to illustrate your description.

B. Through the ages, we have been waiting for Jesus to return. Read the story of October 22, 1844, found in the TRM. Research other stories and details surrounding this day. Choose a method to present the information.

C. Plan a reunion in heaven of those who followed Jesus when He was on this earth. What might they say to Jesus? What would you like to say or ask?

D. Write a letter to a friend explaining the three kinds of salvation and the relationship of justification and sanctification to glorification.

To Learn More

The Bible Pageant (1986), vol. 5, pp. 160–163
The Bible Story, vol. 10, pp. 167–170, 196–200
Early Writings, pp. 13–20

ACKNOWLEDGMENTS

Grateful acknowledgment is made to the following members who served at various times on the Elementary Bible Textbook Steering Committee during the development and writing of *Becoming Like Him: God's Reflection.*

Joan Davis
Tim Fisher
Debra Fryson
Linda Gertz
Erma Lee
Allayne Martsching
Laura Mayne
Joy Veverka

Special acknowledgment is given to the following people who made significant contributions:

Marion Hartlein
Gerald Kovalski
Carol Pack

Pacific Press® Publishing Association
Paul Hey
Bonnie Tyson-Flyn

Design and Layout
Genesis Design/Bryan Gray

Grateful acknowledgment is made to the following publisher for permission to use copyrighted materials.

Scriptures quoted from the *Student's Life Application Bible, New Living Translation,* copyright 2004, 1997, 1994, 1992 by Tyndale House Publishers, Inc., Wheaton, Illinois. Used by permission.

Every effort has been made to trace the ownership of all copyrighted materials in this book and to obtain permission for its use.

Sincere appreciation is given to the many others who have contributed to the manuscript whose names may not be included.